ALL PAKISTAN PREMIERE TOMORROW

FILMARTS *present* ZEBA . WAHEED in

ARMAAN

I0143294

A VERY SPECIAL MOTION PICTURE

WITH

TARANNUM · ROZINA · BIBBO · NIRALA & AGHASARWAR

PRODUCED BY	DIRECTED BY	MUSIC
WAHEED MURAD	PERVEZ MALIK	SOHAIL RANA

NAZ — KHAYYAM — SUPER — FIRDOUS — SHALIMAR — NAGINA —
(Kesmari)
CHAMAN — GULZAR — GULISTAN — IMPERIAL — SHIRIN — SHIRIN
(Malir) (Landhi) (Drigh Rd.) (Korangi) (New Karachi)
ELITE — ODEON — CHIRAGHMAHAL
(Lattiabad)

About the Author

Khurram Ali Shafique is an historian and educationist, and the author of biographies, screenplays and numerous articles in English and Urdu languages. He is the founding director of the Marghdeen Iqbal Studies Centre, which offers online courses on Iqbal's philosophy.

Shafique's publications include *2017: The Battle for Marghdeen* (2012), *The Republic of Rumi: A Novel of Reality* (2007), *Samandar Ki Awaz Suno* (Urdu, 1993) and a series of six biographies of Iqbal in Urdu, three of which have been published so far. He wrote the TV movie *Iqbal: An Approach to Pakistan* (2009). His *Iqbal: an Illustrated Biography* (2006) won the Presidential Iqbal Award in 2011, and has since been translated into a number of languages.

Visit Shafique's websites:

Marghdeen Iqbal Studies Centre: www.marghdeen.com
Waheed Murad: www.waheedmurad.com

Waheed Murad
His Life
and
Our Times

Khurram Ali Shafique

Libredux

Copyright © 2015 Khurram Ali Shafique

The author asserts the moral right to be
identified as the author of this work

A catalogue record for this book is
available from the British Library

This is a work of non-fiction. Names, characters, places and events are not
the product of the author's imagination – although some might be the product
of those artists and writers to whom they have been credited in the book. Any
resemblance to actual persons living or dead
is not coincidental (we hope!).

All rights reserved. Printed in the United Kingdom and the
United States of America. No part of this publication may be reproduced,
stored in a retrieval system, or transmitted, in any form or by any means,
electronic, mechanical, photocopying, recording, or otherwise, without the
prior written permission of the publisher and/or the author, except in the case
of reviewers who may quote brief passages in a review.

Waheed Murad: His Life and Our Times
http://www.waheedmurad.com

UK/US edition
ISBN: 978-0-9571416-7-4

UK/US edition published by
Libredux Publishing, Nottingham

http://www.libredux.com

Contents

اگر می آید آں دانائے رازے
بدہ اُو را نوائے دلگدازے
ضمیرِ اُمتّاں را می کند پاک
کلیمے یا حکیمے نَے نوازے

If that Knower of the Secret comes,
Give him a song that wins the hearts.
For the souls of nations are purified
Either by a Moses, or by a philosopher who plays on the flute.

Prayer of Allama Dr. Sir Muhammad Iqbal
on his deathbed, 1938

Waheed Murad (1938-1983)

Prologue

A Question

In August 1588, the Spanish Armada invaded England with a fleet of 130 ships. It is generally believed now that its defeat was indecisive in strategic terms but became a great propaganda victory for England. The Latin inscription on the commemorative medal is usually translated as 'God blew with His wind and they were scattered.'[1] The British believed that God favoured the Protestant cause, and out of this feeling was born a sense of national pride that expressed itself partially through an unprecedented growth of vernacular theatre. William Shakespeare had made his debut just a little earlier but became popular soon after the defeat of the Armada.

There appears to be a parallel in the history of Pakistan. In September 1965, the Indian invasion involved some of the largest deployments of tanks since the Second World War – and hence comparable to the Spanish fleet of the sixteenth century. The outcome of the war, indecisive in strategic terms, boosted the morale of the people of Pakistan. The local film industry suddenly reached an unprecedented high, which lasted for almost two decades – just like the boom in the English theatre after the Armada.

In England, theatre was eventually shut down by a puritanical regime, and the demise of the film industry in Pakistan is also sometimes linked with the Islamization policies of General Zia-ul-Haque (although this might not be completely true).

---

[1] 'Flavit Jehovah et Dissipati Sunt'.

Half a century later, there happens to be a consensus on who should be the symbol of the Pakistani film industry of that bygone era. It is the actor-writer-producer-director Waheed Murad. Whether his work deserves serious attention has yet to be decided – just as it was a matter of dispute even about Shakespeare for a very long time. In the preface of the complete works of Shakespeare published in 1725, Alexander Pope complained that Shakespeare's plays were for the amusement of the least refined of the audience, and Shakespeare could not have cherished artistic ideals when his mind was set on commercial success. For a hundred and fifty years, the best minds of England attempted to 'improve' the plays of Shakespeare by re-writing them for the stage, not unlike the 're-makes' now being attempted of some classic movies in Pakistan. History seems to be repeating itself but as we have heard from a very famous lion in a very famous book (and film), 'Things never happen the same way twice.'[1]

Waheed Murad: His Life and Our Times is therefore a bid to make the difference.

The people of England took their playwright seriously after they had won an empire. Can the people of Pakistan do it the other way around, and find through recent heritage the much-needed confidence in their existence as a people? This is the question I hope to answer in this book.

I offer my special thanks to the family of Waheed Murad, especially Mrs. Salma Murad and Adil Murad, who often went out of their way for providing me with much-needed information.

I would also like to express my gratitude to those illustrious colleagues, friends and relatives of the subject who allowed me to interview them at various times during the last few decades: Pervez Malik (late), Sohail Rana, Javid Ali Khan, Mariam Issa, Qaisar Mahmood (late), Syed Iqbal Hussain Rizvi, Nisar

---

[1] The allusion is to *The Chronicles of Narnia: Prince Caspian* by C. S. Lewis and the movie based on it.

Bazmi (late), Syed Afzal Hussain (late), Lehri (late), Nirala (late), Asif Noorani, Qadir Moosani, Charlie Anwar, Film Star Aaliya and others.

It is a pleasure to acknowledge my debt to my friend Akhtar Wasim Dar, who helped me in extraordinary ways in my researches. The insights he has shared about the matters discussed in the book are so numerous that they cannot be referenced individually. Instead, I would say that many of the ideas presented here have evolved out of my discussions with Dar.

Syed Zafar Khurshid, the administrator of the Facebook page, 'Waheed Murad, the Superstar' generously invited me to his collection of resources, upon which I have drawn freely. I thank him earnestly. The URL of his page is www.facebook.com/WaheedMuradTheSuperstar

I also want to thank Namrah Mahmood, the writer of the blog *The Caravan of Light,* for her excellent synopses of several movies of Waheed, which were extremely helpful in writing my commentaries in Chapters 2 and 3.

Fareed Ashraf Ghazi and Guddu Khan are fans of Waheed whom I could not meet in person but from whose work I have benefited. I have also made extensive use of the website 'Mazhar.dk' and it is my pleasure to acknowledge my special debt to its creator, Mazhar Iqbal.

Other resources have been mentioned duly in the book. On some occasions I had to rely on my memory about articles that were read long time ago but could not be accessed again at this time. The responsibility for the accuracy of such citations is entirely mine. I have tried to indicate them as much as possible, hoping that some other research scholar will make these and other primary sources widely available in well-edited anthologies sometime in the near future.

It is also my pleasure to acknowledge my debt to my friend Akhtar Wasim Dar helped me in extraordinary ways in my researches, and also shared numerous insights about the matters discussed in the book.

Khurram Ali Shafique

May 2015

Coventry, UK

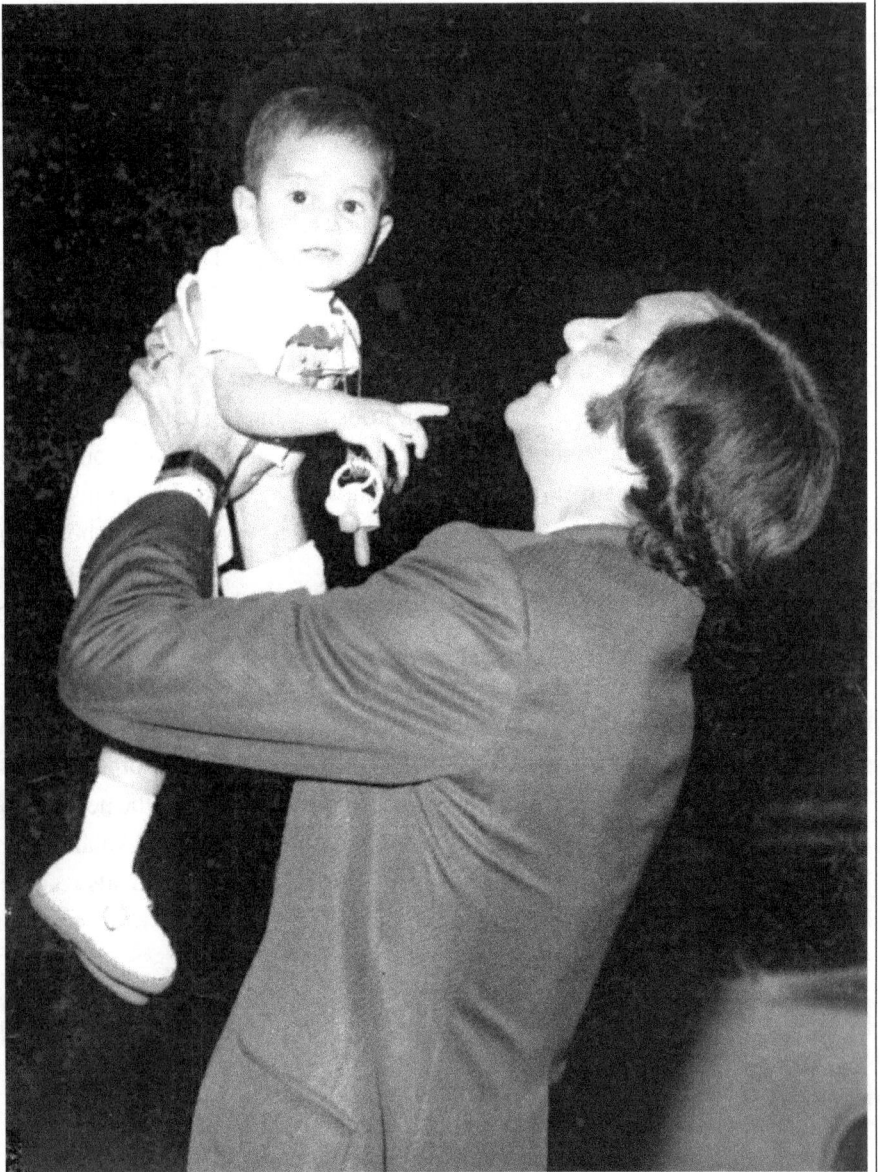

Waheed Murad with his son, Adil

Chapter 1
The Man Behind the Legend

T he ancestors of Waheed Murad were once near royalty in the Bahmani Kingdom of South India. Sometime after the disintegration of the kingdom in 1517, they migrated to Kashmir on invitation of the ruler of that state. Subsequently they became known as the New Bahmani family.[1]

Kashmir was a world-renowned centre of culture and learning at that time, aptly called *Iran-i-Saghir*, or 'the mini-Iran' but conditions began deteriorating in the late eighteenth century. The New Bahmani family had to migrate again, this time to the city of Sialkot in Punjab. One of them, Sheikh Karam Ilahi, became especially influential in the new city sometime in the nineteenth century, and was known as 'Raise-i-Azam.'[2] His house was called Karam Lodge. The family was also in possession of other real estate, including a garden called Sheikhan da Bagh and a well that was named Babay dee Bairi.[3]

Sheikh Zahoor Ilahi Murad, the grandfather of Waheed, was born in 1887. He and his younger siblings – Feroz-ud-Din, Khurshid Begum, Ahmad Bibi,

---

[1] My source of information for the history of the Murad family is the late Commodore (retired) Qaisar Mahmood, a grandson of Zahoor Ilahi Murad, whom I interviewed at his residence in Lahore on September 12, 2013; and exchanged a few emails the same month. He very kindly went through the first draft of the relevant portion and checked it for accuracy.

[2] According to the late Qaisar Mahmood, this was written on the gravestone of Karam Ilahi.

[3] According to the late Qaisar Mahmood, the pedigree was written on a wall in Karam Lodge. The oldest name in the list was some Fateh Muhammad.

Meher Ilahi and Fazal Ilahi – were the first generation in the family to have Murad as their last names. The reason is unknown. Last names were not necessarily the family names in South Asia in those days. Since 'Murad' literally means 'wish' in Persian, it could be that the birth of Zahoor answered some special prayer of his parents. In the Sufi tradition, which prevailed in the region, 'murad' also meant a disciple chosen by God to become the epitome of Unity. In the mundane world, it was the most common name among the Ottoman rulers of Turkey, who were still regarded highly by Muslims even in South Asia.[1]

Sheikh Zahoor Ilahi Murad received his early education at Scotch Mission School, Sialkot. One of his teachers in that institution was Maulvi Syed Mir Hasan, now best remembered as the mentor of Allama Dr. Sir Muhammad Iqbal (who completed his primary school exam the year Zahoor was born). Mir Hasan was a celebrity in his own right as well. He was an ardent supporter of the great reformer Sir Syed Ahmad Khan. He was also among the founding members of Mohammedan Educational Conference, the predecessor of the All-India Muslim League as the representative organization of the Indian Muslim community.[2]

Maulvi Syed Mir Hasan

---

[1] Syed Sulaiman Nadvi (Urdu; 1922), pp.84, etc.

[2] For a detailed biography of Maulvi Syed Mir Hasan, see Dr. Sultan Mahmood Husain (Urdu; 1981).

Zahoor became prominent among the pupils of Maulvi Hasan and has been mentioned as such in the biography of that great teacher.[1] He studied law and became an advocate by profession. His younger brother, Feroz-ud-Din Murad, pursued Physics and became renowned as F. D. Murad, at one time the head of the Physics Department at the Aligarh Muslim University (originally the Mohammedan Anglo-Oriental College founded by Sir Syed). The university still offers an F. D. Murad Imamuddin Medal for first position in M. Sc. (Physics).[2] One of the writings of F. D. Murad on modern science was also included in a textbook of Urdu compiled in the 1920's by Iqbal and his disciple Hakeem Ahmed Shuja. The youngest brother of Zahoor, Sheikh Fazal Ilahi, was the father of Anwar Murad, who became a senior officer in Pakistan Navy and later served as the ambassador of Pakistan in Turkey and Sri Lanka.

Zahoor was at one time the legal advisor to the Queen of Bhopal.[3] Back in his native city, his philanthropic bent of mind compelled him to serve needy clients for free. He also participated in campaigns against social vices, such as alcohol and prostitution, which were generally resented by the residents as the undesirable influence of the British garrison.

Not surprisingly, he wanted his children to serve the community through education. His eldest son, Zafar, graduated from Murray College, Jammu, and spent his life teaching in the schools of Anjuman Himayat-i-Islam (a leading grass root organization of the South Asian Muslim community) before retiring as a head master. Zahoor's daughter Anwari Murad joined the same profession and retired as Vice Principal of Mission Girls High School, Sialkot.

In his later years, Zahoor had to suffer a personal tragedy. His youngest child, Nazeer Ahmad, developed tuberculosis while still in his teens. He was sent to a sanatorium in the hilly environs of Abbottabad in the North-West Frontier Province. Against the backdrop of serene mountains, and while suffering from the as-yet-incurable disease, he fell in love with a woman from the lower class. Zahoor could not allow this match, and the young boy died soon afterwards at the young age of seventeen. Here was a real-life love story,

---

[1] Dr. Sultan Mahmood Husain (Urdu; 1981),
[2] It is listed among medals distributed in the most recent convocation held on October 16, 2014. See References.
[3] The Queen was regarded as one of the leaders of the 'national Renaissance of Muslim India' and single-handedly funded the entire research project about the life of the Holy Prophet undertaken by the renowned historian Shibli Numani. The outcome was the multi-volume *Seeratun Nabi (The Life of the Prophet),* which is usually regarded as the greatest biography of the Prophet ever written.

not unlike some of the later-day movies in which the yet-to-be-born nephew of the deceased was going to portray similar roles.

The mystical stoicism of Zahoor's nature could be observed during the funeral of his son. Walking beside the coffin, he kept expressing gratitude to the Almighty. To someone who showed surprise at this, he explained, 'What could I have done if God had taken away my son seventeen minutes after birth? Or seventeen months? I am grateful that he was allowed to be with me for seventeen years.'

This was sometime in the late 1930's. Around the same time, Zahoor's second youngest son, Nisar, left home for Bombay. Apparently this was because Zahoor did not have much of an inheritance to pass on to his children. In spite of a successful career in law, he had spent too much time in philanthropic pursuits and community service.

Nisar had been born in Sialkot on June 7, 1915.[1] It is believed that he left the city in the late 1930's. He had either fallen in love with cinema already or developed this passion soon after arriving in Bombay (now Mumbai), the biggest centre of movie production in British India (with Calcutta and Lahore ranking behind it). In Bombay, he soon found a job with a film distribution company, India Films Bro.

Like the Elizabethans of Shakespeare's times, the Muslim middle class in the British India also looked down upon performing arts, and Nisar's father may have disapproved this choice of profession.[2]

Back in Bombay, Nisar had met a Christian woman from Bikaner (Rajasthan), working here as a nurse. She converted to Islam, was renamed

---

[1] This is written on his passports (cited in References), now in the possession of his grandson, Adil Murad. The same date of birth is displayed on his gravestone in the Gulberg Graveyard, Lahore (his grave is near his son's).

[2] His views are not known. According to the late Qaisar Mahmood, other members of the Murad family later resented the family name becoming associated with cinema.

A public statement of Iqbal from the 1930s: "If such films could be produced in India which do not promote sinfulness and impiety but aim at rendering true service to the country and awakening the real emotions in the youth; presenting some high standard of morality; [and] which are intended to promote the pure thoughts of love for the homeland, indeed such films can be very useful for the land and its people. If such a company comes forward with this lofty ambition, it will indeed render a service to the land." Source: Dr. Sir Muhammad Iqbal (Urdu; 1967/1977), p.295.

Shirin and married Nisar. They moved to Karachi as Nisar was posted to the branch of the company there.

The only child of Nisar and Shirin was Waheed Murad, born in Karachi on October 2, 1938. It is said that he was first given the name Waheed Ahmad since the family was not using the surname Murad at that time, due to fallout between Zahoor and his brother F. D. Murad. According to this report, Nisar also went by the name of Nisar Ahmad in those days and the surname Murad was reclaimed only after a reconciliation.[1]

That was after the death of Zahoor Ilahi Murad, who passed away in Sialkot on November 10, 1938. If local newspapers carried the news, it may have been pushed aside a little by the obituary of Mustafa Kemal Ataturk, who died on the same day in Turkey.

---

[1] According to the late Qaisar Mahmood, Zahoor stopped giving his children the surname Murad after the firstborn, Zafar Ilahi Murad. Others were named Qamar Mahmood, Anwari Mahmood (female), Saleem Mahmood, Kalim Mahmood, Salima Akhtar (female), Nasim Ahmad, Nisar Ahmad and Nazeer Ahmad. They reverted to the family name after reconciliation with the children of F. D. Murad, which happened after the death of Zahoor.

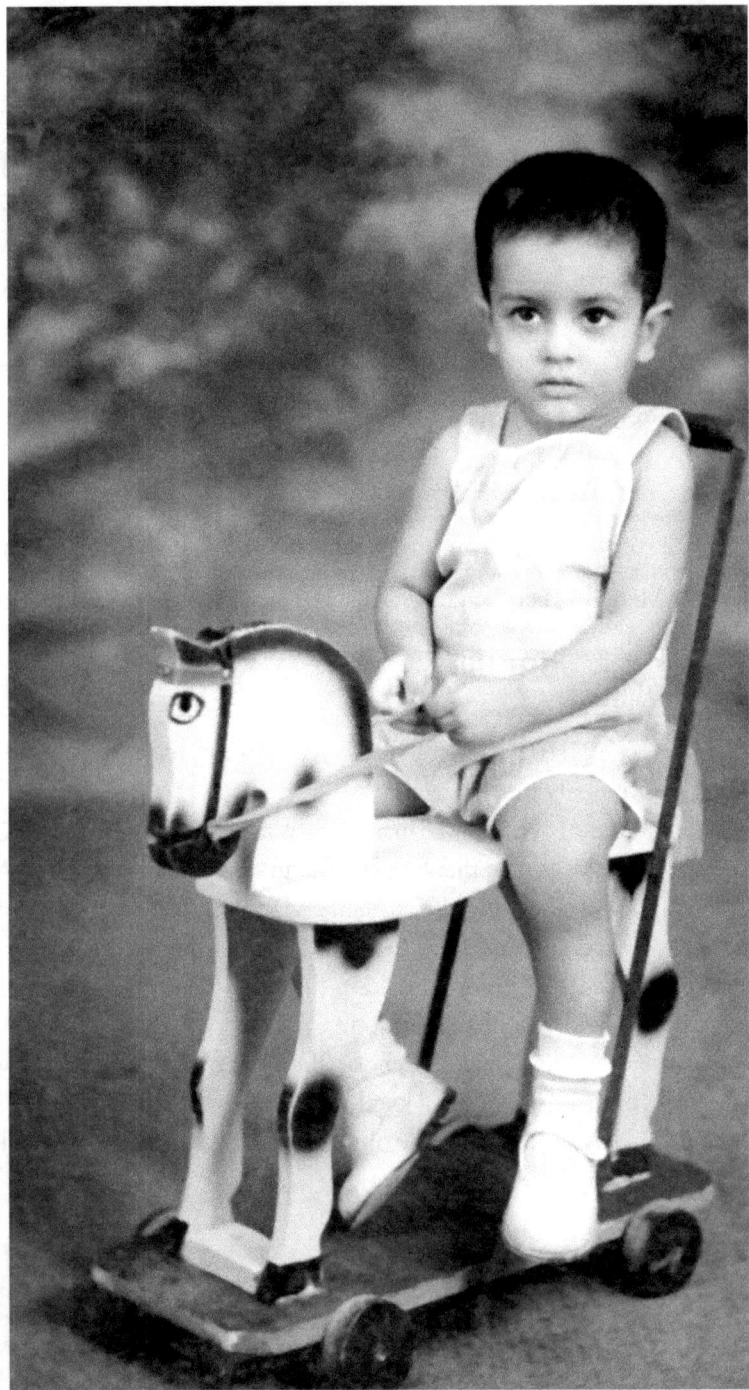

Waheed Murad: possibly his first encounter with the camera

The education of Waheed is said to have started at Lawrence College, Murree Hills.[1] More than 1,500 kilometres away from Karachi, it remains one of the most prestigious educational institutions in the region, established by the British in 1860. Schooling is offered for grades 1 to 12, divided into Junior School (Grades 1-4), Prep School (Grades 5-7) and Senior School (Grades 8-12). Most students stay in hostels, which are separate for each school. The average age for intake in Grade 1 is five plus, and since the term starts in March, Waheed may have joined the Junior School in March 1944.

In addition to the Victorian era buildings of the hostel and classrooms, and a church, there was also a Christian cemetery at that time, which completed an ambience very similar to that of Yorkshire in England. The influence is discernible in the movie *Armaan,* written by Waheed some twenty years later with allusions to *Wuthering Heights* and *Jane Eyre,* the famous works by the Brontë sisters that are set against the backdrop of Victorian Yorkshire.

Although he kept coming back to Murree, his initial stay at Lawrence College was short because his parents took him back quickly. They had found it difficult to be separated from their only child.[2]

In Karachi, he was sent to Marie Colaco School in the Saddar Cantonment (just behind the Empress Market, also a landmark of the Victorian architecture). Pronounced 'Co-la-so', the school was among the leading educational institutions and received intake from the elite of the city. Like Lawrence College, it was also run by a European management.

Being the son of a film distributor meant that the formal education received at school was non-formally supplemented by cinema, even when the vernacular movies were not something to boast about from the perspective of the elitist education imparted at the school.

For six out of the first seven years of his life, the world around him was engaged in war. The Second World War started in 1939 and lasted till 1945, although the experience was understandably different in Karachi from that in

---

[1] Reported to the author by Javid Ali Khan.
[2] Reported to the author by Javid Ali Khan.

Europe, the Americas or other scenes of conflict. Under the legendary mayor Jamshed Nusserwanjee Mehta, Karachi was still the cleanest city in Asia.

Yet those were not the times to remain impartial – even for kids. A homeland envisioned by Iqbal in 1930 became the demand of the Indian Muslims in 1940, led by their Quaid-i-Azam ('the Great Leader'), Muhammad Ali Jinnah, who stood equally firm in the face of bitter opposition from the Hindus and condescending resentment from the British. Some of his personality traits, especially highlighted in a famous account written by the British journalist Beverley Nichols, were later going to become the hallmark of Waheed, such as an elegant taste in dress and a restrained manner of speech:

> Jinnah had been almost brutally critical of British policy ..., but his criticism had been clear and creative. It was not merely a medley of wild words, a hotchpotch of hatred and hallucination, in the Hindu manner. It was more like a diagnosis. The difference between Jinnah and the typical Hindu politician was the difference between a surgeon and a witch doctor. Moreover, he was a surgeon you could trust, even though his verdict was harsh.
>
> 'The British must realize,' he said to me before we tackled the problem of Pakistan, 'that they have not a friend in the country. Not a friend.'
>
> A Hindu politician would have said that at the top of his voice, with delight. Jinnah said it quietly, with regret.[1]

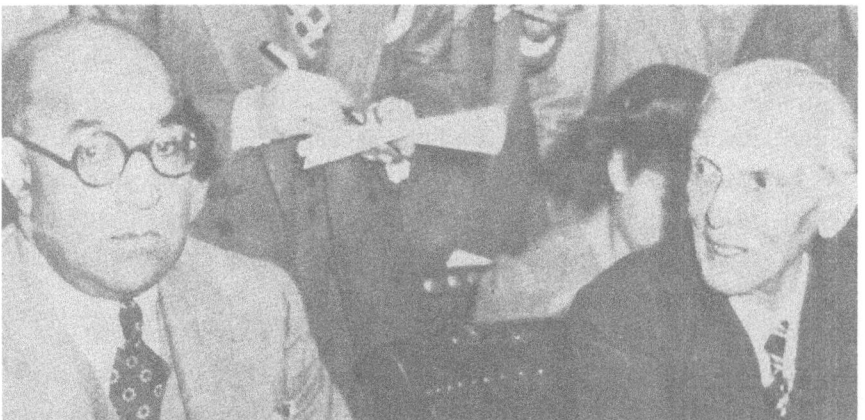

Quaid-i-Azam Muhammad Ali Jinnah, founder and the first Governor-General of Pakistan (right) with Quaid-i-Millat Liaquat Ali Khan, the first prime minister (left)

[1] Beverley Nichols (1944), pp.191-192

This difference between Jinnah and other Indian leaders, emphasized here by Nichols, was later going to find a parallel in how Waheed would be distinguished as an actor: 'famous for his charming expressions, attractive personality, tender voice...'[1]

Pakistan came into being on the midnight between August 14 and 15, 1947, and Waheed must have witnessed the festivities, especially as Karachi became the capital city of the new state (and remained so till 1959). The Quaid arrived on August 7, sovereignty was transferred by the Viceroy to the Constituent Assembly on August 14, and the birth of the state was celebrated the next morning.[2]

With the partition of the British India, the film distribution network of Nisar Murad also became independent of its head office in India and was renamed Pakistan Films.[3]

The young Waheed – 'Veedu', as he was called by those who were close to him – was a witness to rapid transformation of landscape, demography and the world around him. New friends arrived in school – including Javid Ali Khan, a nephew one step removed of the Prime Minister, who became a fast friend of Waheed; and Pervez Malik, the son of an army officer, whom Waheed would later introduce as one of the most patriotic film directors in the history of the country.

Pervez later wrote:

---

[1] This description appeared in the Wikipedia entry about him retrieved on November 14, 2014 from http://en.wikipedia.org/wiki/Waheed_Murad
[2] The sovereignty of the constituent assembly was later denied in a court ruling by Chief Justice Muhammad Munir in 1955, but I am following the opinion of Justice (later Chief Justice) R. A. Cornelius. In his dissenting note, he asserted that sovereignty had been transferred to the constituent assembly of Pakistan at the time of independence. This is corroborated by the speech of the Quaid-i-Azam delivered in the inaugural session of the assembly on August 11, 1947, in which the assembly was addressed as a sovereign body, and this is how matters were generally understood before the 1955 verdict of Justice Munir.
[3] Reported to the author by the late Qaisar Mahmood.

21

Nisar and Shirin Murad (front left) and Waheed (back middle) with others

I took admission in that school when my father got posted to Karachi in 1949. That is where I met Waheed for the first time. We were both studying in Class IV. I lived in an apartment near Saeed Manzil on Bunder Road [M. A. Jinnah Road] and Waheed also lived in an apartment a little ahead on Bunder Road in front of Light House Cinema. One day he offered me lift in his car which I accepted happily and this was the beginning of our friendship. Waheed, whom we lovingly called 'Weedu', was a very bright student and was especially ahead of the class in English. In sports he was much fond of cricket and we both were members of the cricket team in our school. We participated in many matches.[1]

From the residence on M. A. Jinnah Road, mentioned here, the family later moved to 231-C, Block 2, P. E. C. H. Society, and then some time after April 1965, to 158-R, Tariq Road, Block 2, P.E.C.H. Society.[2]

---

[1] Obituary of Waheed Murad by Pervez Malik in Urdu, anthologized in S. A. Najam (Urdu; n.d.), pp.64-75

[2] The first address appears on the passport of Nisar Murad issued in April 1965, and is changed to the latter on p.6 at the time of the passport's renewal on June 8, 1970.

High School Final Examination, 1954 .

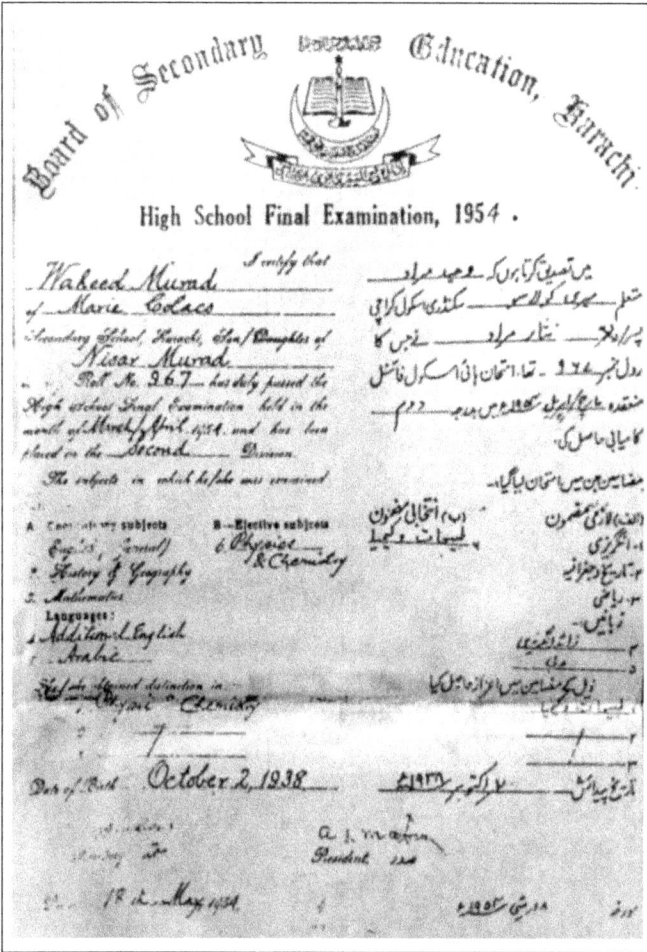

W a h e e d passed the High School Final Examination (the 'Matric') in 1954, with Arabic and Additional English as optional languages, and distinction in Physics and Chemistry. He then took admission in S. M. Science College but after passing the Intermediate Examination in science he opted for humanities and passed the Bachelor of Arts (B.A.) from S. M. Arts College.[1]

By this point, both he and Pervez had applied to the University of California, Los Angeles, to study filmmaking. They received the admission papers, but Nisar and Shirin could not reconcile with the thought of separating from their only child for three years.

They suggested that Waheed should set up his own production company and learn filmmaking through hands-on experience. This could be supplemented by studying English Literature at Karachi University (as an external candidate, since he would also be running his production house).[2]

---

[1] Obituary of Waheed Murad by Pervez Malik in Urdu, anthologized in S. A. Najam (Urdu; n.d.), pp.64-75
[2] Obituary of Waheed Murad by Pervez Malik in Urdu, anthologized in S. A. Najam (Urdu; n.d.), pp.64-75

A trip to Murree was usually undertaken every summer with Javid Ali Khan and other friends.[1] The parents would give the boys a lump sum amount and leave it up to them to make the budget. The boys preferred to pool in the money and book an apartment so that they could stay for a longer duration, rather than go for the convenience of a hotel and end up with a shorter stay.

Javid was a regular student at the Department of English Literature at Karachi University and shared his class notes with Waheed, who was an external candidate. Waheed also participated in extracurricular activities at the university and the prize he received in an elocution competition was the novel, *Ulysses* by James Joyce. It became his favourite reading as he was thrilled by

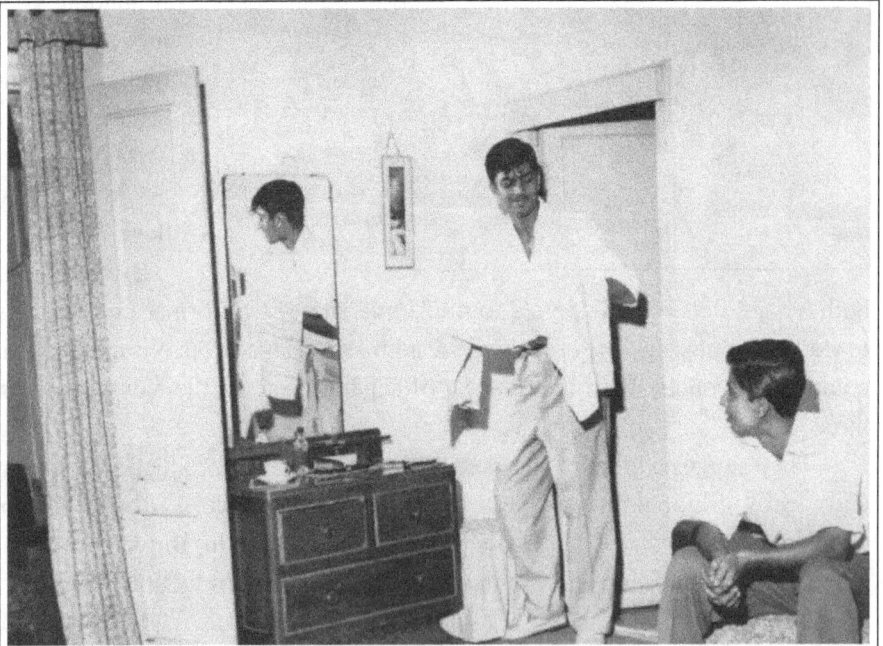

Waheed with a friend in the 1950s

---

[1] Reported to the author by Javid Ali Khan.

The 1960s: Waheed (third from left) and Javid Ali Khan (third from right)

'the extended use of the unspoken soliloquy or silent monologue, an exact transcription of the stream of consciousness of the individual, which certainly has the air of an untouched photographic record and has, indeed, been compared to the film of a moving picture'.[1] He also familiarized himself with other users of this technique, including Henry James, Virginia Woolf and William Faulkner. An idea which he often discussed with Javid in those days was to employ this in a mainstream Pakistani film (and it seems that he later did that in *Ishara*).[2]

He was coming out as an avid collector of books, and apart from the stream of consciousness novels he also collected works of and about modern drama, and bestsellers.[3]

To Javid, Waheed appeared to be marked for success in any profession that he would choose. He was unusually intelligent and brought finesse to everything he did, be it the organizing of a cricket match with friends or a venture of business.

---

[1] This description of the stream of consciousness narrative mode is taken from Stuart Gilbert (1955), pp.10-11, because it was widely acclaimed at that time and hence Waheed may have known about it. In more modern terms, it is 'a technique which seeks to record the flow of impressions passing through a character's mind.' Peter Childs & Roger Fowler (2006), p.224

[2] My source of information for this and other activities of Waheed Murad during his university days is Javid Ali Khan.

[3] Mrs. Habib (n.d.); quoted later in this chapter.

His other distinguishing feature, according to Javid, was his immense sensitivity and empathy for the suffering of others. Javid suffered an emotional setback in those days and shared it with Waheed. The next day, when he visited Waheed's house, he saw him in tears before his mother who was trying to console him. As Waheed left the room and Javid asked Waheed's mother why Waheed was crying, it turned out that he was only telling her about what Javid was going through.[1]

Waheed launched his production house in 1960 by the name of Film Arts. Hence his profession would be stated as 'Film Producer Artist' in his passport – along with personal details such as 5′ 8″ height; dark brown eyes; and black hair.[2] To such personal trivia could be added later, Paco Rabanne Pour Homme as Waheed's favourite perfume after it was introduced by Jean Martel in 1973.[3]

Waheed became the youngest film producer in the history of the country with the release of his first production, *Insaan Badalta Hai,* the next year. This was followed by *Jabse Dekha Hai Tumhen* in 1963. He did not act in either of these movies. However, he made an

Waheed as a young man

---

[1] Reported to the author by Javid Ali Khan
[2] Passport cited in References.
[3] Reported to the author by Mrs. Salma Murad

Film stars Alla-ud-din (left) and Talish (right) with Waheed.

uncredited cameo appearance in *Saathi* (1959) and a proper debut in *Aulad* (1962), followed by *Daaman* (1963). In both the latter films, he played supporting roles but received great critical acclaim. Eventually he decided to appear as the lead in his next production.

Movies were being produced in Karachi since 1955, when the city became the second centre of film production after Lahore. Dacca (now Dhaka) in East Pakistan had followed a year later. In Karachi, Eastern Film Studios in the SITE area boasted two large floors, huge open spaces and modern equipment.[1] This is where Waheed would produce his films, except the last three.

He came out as a thorough businessman from the very start. Film trade never gained the status of an industry in Pakistan during his lifetime. As such, films could not be insured. Producers were notorious for withholding payments, especially of the lower staff but sometimes also of the minor stars. Some, especially newcomers, squandered away their budgets on extracurricular activities and left the project unfinished. Waheed entered the business as one of those few who were miles apart from this culture. In monetary matters he was tight-fisted like a cool-headed businessman but was also extremely honest, upright and reliable. Payments were made out by him without reminders, and he extended professional respect even to the lower staff. Other than this he was aloof and shy to the point of being mistaken as arrogant.[2] The comedian Lehri described him aptly as 'a to-the-point man, well-educated and noble'.[3]

---

[1] Asif Noorani 'Those were the days'. See References.
[2] Reported to the author by Syed Iqbal Hussain Rizvi.
[3] Statement in the PTV show *Silver Jubilee* (1983). Retrieved from YouTube on

The M. A. exams were held in May 1962. Some time after that Waheed was on a long drive with Javid at night when the jeep developed some fault. They were quite far away from Karachi and were told that the caretaker of a Sufi shrine in a nearby town has a similar jeep, so his driver might be able to help them. The name of the town was given to them as Sehwan, and the shrine was that of Lal Shahbaz Qalandar.

University of Karachi

FACULTY OF ARTS
Master of Arts

Whereas _____ WAHEED MURAD _____

has pursued a course of study prescribed by this University for the Degree of Master of Arts in ENGLISH in the Faculty of Arts and has passed the requisite examination held in VIII 19 62, having been placed in SECOND class.

It is hereby certified that he/she has been duly admitted to the degree of **Master of Arts** *in this University at the Convocation of 19 63.*

Registrar _____ *Vice-Chancellor*

Dated Karachi the 17th MAY 1963.

The real name of the saint was Syed Muhammad Usman Marwandi, and he was born in 1177 in the Persian town of Marand. This was not far from Tabriz, from where the famous Shams hailed at the same time, who would later become the mentor of Maulana Jalaluddin Rumi. After travelling around the Muslim world, he settled at Sehwan in Sindh, where he taught Muslim jurisprudence and ran a monastery of the Suhrawardi order of Sufism, and died in 1274. He was the author of at least four books, covering the subjects of Islamic jurisprudence and Sufism. He was a close friend of Baha-ud-Din Zakariya of Multan, Fariduddin Ganjshakkar of Pakpattan and Syed Jalaluddin Bukhari of Uch. In popular culture, the folk song 'Damadam mast Qalandar' was dedicated to him and identified him with the mythical 'Jhoolay Lal', revered by the Hindus of Sindh. Just as the dance of the whirling dervishes was

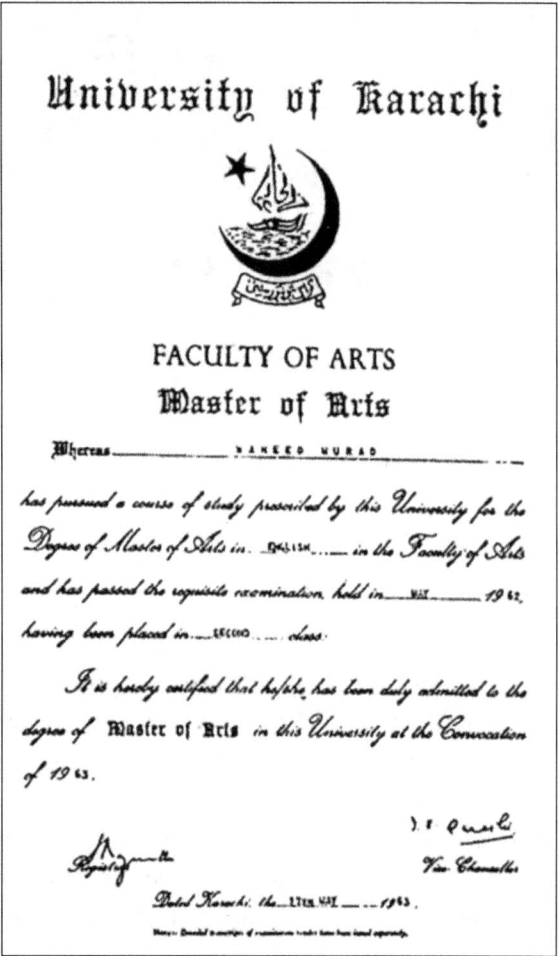

November 17, 2014: http://www.youtube.com/watch?v=IO9CJ3eVp_Q

performed at the mausoleum of Rumi, the devotional dance of *dhammal* was associated with the shrine of Shahbaz.

Both Javid and Waheed were interested in Sufism but neither of them had heard about the Qalandar of Sehwan before. They arrived at the shrine at a late hour but the caretaker received them courteously and after listening to their story he said that they may have been summoned by the spirit of the Qalandar. He advised them to visit the grave, offer fateha and pray to God for any wish which they wanted to come true. They did accordingly and spent the night as guests. In the morning, the driver was asked to fix the jeep. He recognized Waheed from his acting roles and was quite happy to be of help. They returned after visiting the grave once again.

On the way back, Javid told Waheed that he had prayed for a first division in M.A. He then asked Waheed what did he wish for. Waheed replied, 'I prayed that I become the greatest superstar of Pakistan.'

The results of M.A. were announced soon afterwards. Javid got his first division. Waheed got second divisions, just a few marks short of the first.[1] The degree was issued on May 17, 1963.

By then, Waheed had made up his mind to get married. His choice was Salma Maker, the daughter of E. H. A. Maker – a leading industrialist and the owner of H. M. Silk Mills. In her own words:

> Waheed and I were childhood friends. Never did I ever think that I would be married to him. He was seriously involved with my best friend (she is no more in this world now). She and I were both studying in the St. Lawrence's convent in Karachi. During our lunch break we used to go over to his house which was not very far off. Once we were late for our French classes and were punished and made to stand out of our class for the whole period. Next time we made sure we reached our class in time.

---

[1] The anecdote was related to the author by Javid Ali Khan.

Waheed and Salma Murad

His next love interest was also a good friend of mine. Waheed got very serious with her and a proposal was sent to parents. For some reason it did not materialize. Waheed was devastated and depressed, and we all friends used to console him and he used to cry on our shoulders.

I was at that period very much involved with Ghanshyam and Nalima. My father had helped them to set up this academy in P.E.C.H.S and I was one of his first pupils. We were at that moment preparing to go to New York for a performance. After great difficulty I had been allowed to go by my mother (my father was very liberal).

This dance of light and sound by Ghanshyam and myself on a big tabla had taken about a year of rehearsal to prepare. I was very excited and looking forward to going. On the last day of the rehearsal the premises was jam-packed. I was on stage performing. I saw Waheed standing at the gate with a typical look on his face (which you often see on the screen) and staring. I was getting a little nervous and uncomfortable.

After the performance he came up the stage and said, '*Aap zara bahar aa sakti hain?*' ('Can you come out for a moment?). I said, 'No, not at this moment; after the performance.' He went back and again stood at the gate. After the performance he came back again, '*Aap zara bahar aaein aap say baat karni hay.*' ('Please come out, I have to talk to you a little').

When I sat in the car, Waheed was silent and drove the car at a very high speed. He stopped it at the Old Clifton. I asked him, '*Kya hua?*' ('What happened?'). Silent. '*Kya hua, ghar mien koi baat hui?*' ('What happened, has something happened at home?'). Silent. 'For heaven's sake tell me what on earth has happened?' No answer. He was quiet for a moment. Then he turned around and asked me, 'How would you like to spend the rest of your life with me?' I said, 'No way!' I could see all my plans crashing. He turned around the car at a high speed and dropped me home.

Salma accepted eventually. 'I could never ever forget the face of Nalima and Ghanshyam,' she says. 'They were devastated. This sound and dance had taken a year to rehearse. At the last moment nobody could have taken anyone else in my place. The delegation went without me and I think I made the best decision

Top (from left to right): Shirin Murad, Waheed, Salma and Nisar Murad.
Bottom: another picture from the occasion, Salma and Waheed seated in the
middle. Those standing behind include, from left, Pervez Malik (first), Masroor
Anwar (fourth, the shortest in the row) and Sohail Rana (sixth, hand on
Waheed's shoulder).

of my life. Waheed proved to be a good husband, a good father, a good son and a good friend.'[1]

The marriage took place on September 17, 1964. The grand reception was a party to be remembered. One of the features was a singing performance by Nazeer Baig, an aspiring singer who would eventually become the superstar, Nadeem.[2]

Waheed's rise to stardom started with the third production of Film Arts, *Heera Aur Pather* (1964). It was near completion when he got married, and was released soon afterwards. It was his first lead role and he was paired with Zeba. She had also worked in his previous production, *Jabse Dekha Hai Tumhen,* which was her second movie but since then she had become a superstar in her own right – especially with the recently released *Ashiana* (1964).

By now, Pervez Malik had returned with an M.A. in filmmaking from UCLA, and *Heera Aur Pather* was his break as a director. Together with the music director Sohail Rana and the poet Masroor Anwar – both of whom had joined Film Arts with the previous production – they made a marvellous team. Asif Noorani, the editor of the leading film magazine *Eastern Films* at that time, later wrote:

> the one thing which lingers in my memory were the evenings Waheed Murad, director Pervez Malik, writer Masroor Anwar and, every so often, composer Sohail Rana used to spent on the lawns and talk endlessly about films and film craft. I was an occasional participant too. Waheed was very fond of music, a subject which was often discussed, that was when we weren't discussing English literature.[3]

---

[1] Email by Mrs. Salma Murad to the author.
[2] Obituary of Waheed Murad by Pervez Malik in Urdu, anthologized in S. A. Najam (Urdu; n.d.), pp.64-75
[3] Asif Noorani 'Those were the days'. See References.

'I will not say we *influenced* one another,' Sohail was later going to say about the famous four. *'We were one.'*[1] Their remarkable synergy was a practical tribute to the team-building capacity of Waheed, whom the other three acknowledged as a major influence on their professional development.

The movie was a success by all standards. It celebrated a Golden Jubilee at the box office, i.e. 50 cumulative weeks of uninterrupted showing in a regional 'circuit'. This was the highest benchmark of success reached by any Pakistani Urdu film at that time (in those days, the success of movies was measured in the cumulative weeks of running in all the cinemas within a distribution circuit: Silver Jubilee was celebrated for a cumulative run of 25 weeks; Golden Jubilee for 50; Platinum Jubilee for 75 and Diamond Jubilee for 100).[2] No Pakistani Urdu film had ever gone beyond a Golden Jubilee, but Waheed was going to change that with his very next production.

The movie also bagged two Nigar Awards – for Waheed as the best actor and for Aqeel Khan as the best editor. The awards had been introduced by the Urdu film magazine of the same name in 1958, and were seen as the Pakistani equivalent to the Oscar. Waheed was going to receive three more Nigars in his life – best producer for *Armaan* (1966), and best actor for *Andaleeb* (1969) and *Mastana Mahi* (1971) – and one after his death, a lifetime achievement award in 2002. Other awards received in lifetime included five Rooman Awards, three Graduate Awards, two Noor Jahan Awards, two Mussawir Awards, two Sindh Awami Awards, two PIA Arts Academy Awards, two Al-Fankar Awards, two Shabab Awards; and one each of Chitrali, Khalil Qaiser, Curtex, Aghaz, Chaministan International, National, Riaz Shahid and National Academy awards.[3]

Surprisingly, he did not receive patronage from the government in his lifetime – none of those prides of performance, and various stars and crescents that were doled out by dozens every year. Recognition at the state level came posthumously, and only after sustained campaign by his devoted fans, by way of a road named after him Karachi, and a 'Sitara-e-Imtiaz' awarded for lifetime achievement in 2011.

---

[1] Khurram Ali Shafique (1996a)
[2] Waheed celebrated it by distributing a souvenir among the cast and crew: a miniature donkey-cart inscribed with the title of the movie and the words 'Golden Jubilee'. The author saw one in Karachi with the collector of movie memorabilia, Waqar Baig, who acquired it from the film editor Aqeel Khan.
[3] See complete list of awards received by Waheed Murad in appendix.

Waheed and Salma: incidentally, Waheed is wearing the same jacket that he wore in *Armaan* during the Ahmad Rushdi version of the phenomenally famous song, 'Akele na jana'.

A glimpse into the personal life of Waheed in the early days of his stardom is found in a feature about 'modern marriages' published in an English-language magazine some time after the success of *Heera Aur Pather*. The writer was some Mrs. Habib.

MODERN MARRIAGES: SALMA AND WAHEED MURAD
by Mrs. Habib[1]

Dashing Waheed and his demure wife, Salma, need no introduction. The recipient of the Best Actor Award, Waheed is not only a popular screen idol but also the producer of some of the most popular movies made in Pakistan.

The hectic life of a film star, I guess, needs a calm, peaceful home atmosphere, more than any other. That is exactly what you find in their home, a restful atmosphere pervades their living and dining area. No extra piece of decoration, the simplicity of their decor is complemented by wall-to-wall carpet in the most appealing moss green shade, which reminds one of the cool soothing expanse of a golf course.

Some of the items that were outstanding by their beauty were a square low centre table which almost seems to flaunt its perfect streamlined look. An attractive black wrought iron screen, forming a division between the dining and living room area. A book-case takes up one wall, which holds a wide range of books on Modern Drama, short stories and bestsellers. A gigantic wall clock stands on it along with the much coveted Oscar [Nigar] for Best Actor.

Discussing Modern Marriages, Mr. Waheed Murad said that: basically marriage remains the same in past, present or future; the main

---

[1] A scanned copy of the first two pages was provided to the author by Syed Zafar Khurshid. According to him, it is a reprint in some magazine in 1984, but he does not remember the name of the magazine. As evident from the text it must have been printed originally in the late 1965 or the early 1966, i.e. after Waheed had received his first Nigar for *Heera Aur Pather* but before he received the second one for *Armaan*.

difference in today's marriage is that there is an escape route – at one time marriage was for 'till death do us part', the couple accepted their lot and made the best of it. They tried harder to make marriages work. Today the escape route – divorce – is accepted, so that he feels that the slightest bit of trouble makes modern couples think towards this, rather than trying harder, to make their marriage work.

Waheed's wife, Salma, feels that while so many factors go into making marriage successful, a common factor and an important one from time immemorable was the one with the most responsibility resting on the wife, who contributes greatly to the success of a marriage by learning and practising the art of pleasing the husband. This each wife must discover and go out of her way to do.

Waheed described marriage as *'a two way lock, and each partner has one key. Marriage requires give and take as anyone will tell you. But this should not mean, giving up each one's likes and dislikes, but it should mean: readjusting. It should be an honourable compromise for each partner,'* said Waheed.

Talking of the Pakistani modern women, Mr. Waheed said that today a man expects his wife to be part of his business and social life therefore he expects his wife to be presentable. One of the pitfalls of this is, that, this participation in her man's life sometimes exceeds or dominates a wife's life so much that she forgets her basic position.

He feels that today's young woman is far more adaptable, that even the women who

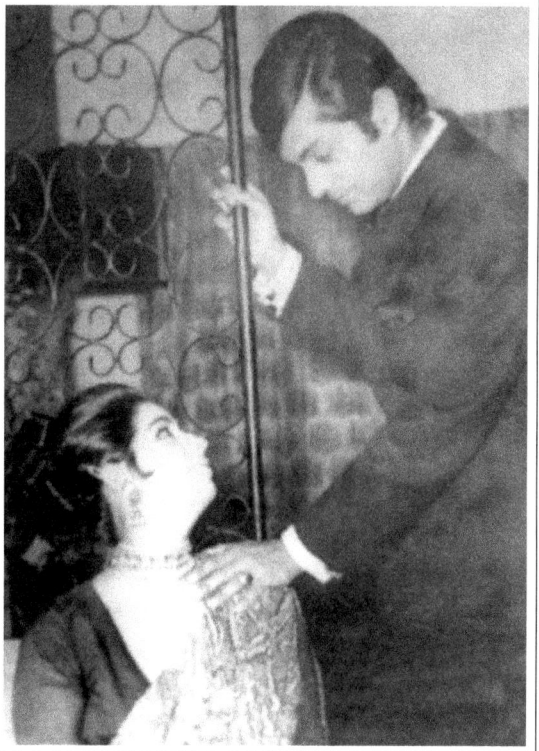

37

come from villages and small towns too, modernize so quickly. Though they do so with great speed, the modernization is usually appropriate, said Waheed. The speed with which the Pakistani women have accepted their roles in modern marriages, modern society, modern professions, etc. can only be described as tremendous, added Waheed.

Salma thinks that the modern young women, who are mostly well educated and of good means, could be doing so much of the much needed social and civic work. She thinks that they should utilize their talent and their education in doing something for other less fortunate people, instead of just wasting their time in frivolous activities all the time.

In reply to my inquiry as to how Salma spent her time, Salma said that she was the member of a social welfare women's club, where she goes once a week. She is also studying Braille, so as to be able to help translate books into Braille, twice a week she has been reading to a blind student for some time now, the student has appeared for his B. A. examinations.

Salma said she enjoys sewing and cooking, she does sewing for her club, where the sewn items are sold and the proceeds given to a deserving cause. Her interest in cooking inspires her to serve something different by way of food at her dinner parties. Waheed and Salma get a rare evening to themselves, when they do, they enjoy reading, playing

cards or playing scrabble.

I asked Salma what had caused obvious change in her style of dressing, since there was a time when Salma was more often flashily dressed than otherwise. She feels that her taste has become subdued, and she said this has been influenced by her spouse, who was ready to take almost all the credit for this change.

Commenting on today's Youth, Waheed Murad said: 'I could not condemn my youth. The age of rebellion comes on all of us, and no one must judge too harshly.' He went on to explain, that when one has so many material possessions, one likes to a whale of a time – and this period seems to be strongest when the young men are going through a period of indecision, about their future career. The young want guidance – but not from any one or everyone – he said.

Waheed went further and said that he thinks, that the young man should that his father or his parents have full trust in him, when he is going through this period of indecision. No one, unless he is an absolute no-good, would willingly let his father down. He says if the parents show this regard for their son's potential, the son will come out alright from this period of aimless merrymaking.

He feels very proud of his own parents who didn't try to enforce him into any particular career, and let him know that they had faith in him. He said, 'I drifted for a time, I tried joining my father's business (his father Mr. Nisar Murad is a film distributor), I didn't find interest in that and got to producing films instead.' He was already a producer of a couple of films while in his final year at college, he is a Master from Karachi University in Literature, his chief interest being Drama.

I inquired where Salma and Waheed had met, and was told that they grew up knowing each other as their families were friends. They had been going on family excursions, picnics, and parties along with the other members of the family, and friends, but it wasn't till a year before their marriage in 1964, that they got interested in each other in a romantic way, and this was perfect, said Waheed, as he feels that a courtship shouldn't last too long as then the glamour wears off.

The next venture of Film Arts, *Armaan,* reflected some of the views expressed by Waheed in this interview, such as a phase of indecision about the future career in the youth, and the matrimonial responsibilities of a modern wife. The story was written by Waheed himself with dialogue and lyrics by Masroor, and screenplay by Pervez. As previously, Pervez also directed the movie while Sohail scored the music. The movie went into production soon after the Indo-Pakistan War of September 1965 and was released in March next year, when the morale of the society was at its highest peak. The success was phenomenal, and words alone may be insufficient to capture the wholeness of the response received from the society. It became the first Pakistani movie to celebrate a Platinum Jubilee, or seventy-five cumulative weeks of uninterrupted showing.[1] All eight songs of the soundtrack, released on gramophone records,

The iconic pose of Zeba and Waheed from the publicity stills of *Armaan*

---

[1] According to a comment posted by Raju Jamil on the Facebook page 'Waheed Murad, the Superstar', the Platinum Jubilee celebration of *Armaan* was held at Jabees Hotel, Karachi.

Advertisement of *Armaan* in the daily *Dawn*

became sensational hits – especially the lilting club song 'Ko ko korina' and the two versions of the love song 'Akele na jana', separately sung by Ahmed Rushdi and Mala. Waheed received the Nigar for best producer. Zeba earned fresh laurels to her already well-established stardom.

Waheed now became the most popular superstar there had ever been in Pakistan. His hairstyle became popular among men from all social backgrounds – wealthy as well as poor, and conservative as well as liberal. Young girls were known to be carrying his picture in their vanity bags.

It also meant that he could not visit public places like before. He had been offering the Friday prayers in the mosque with his friends.[1] Since the chance visit to Sehwan a few years earlier he had also been attending the anniversary of the Qalandar quite regularly every year but when he visited the shrine on the next anniversary, in December, he was spotted by the mammoth crowd of pilgrims. They gathered around him and in spite of his protestations they lifted him onto their shoulders on his way out.

---

[1] Obituary of Waheed Murad by Pervez Malik in Urdu, anthologized in S. A. Najam (Urdu; n.d.), pp.64-75

He may not have envisioned this when he had prayed for stardom at that very spot. He stopped going to places of religious significance after this. As he confided to Pervez (who was with him on this trip), he did not want to be a reason for people to be distracted from the sacred goals.[1]

The 'team' – Waheed, Pervez, Sohail and Masroor – offered two more movies together, and both were released in 1967. They were, *Ehsaan,* the fifth venture of Film Arts; and *Doraha,* produced by Pervez Malik and Sohail Rana under their newly formed banner.

Doraha deserves special attention as a thinly veiled parable about what the four artists were really up to. The story presented the dilemma of an educated young man who chooses a career in music and for this reason his proposal for the daughter of his college professor is turned down. While he argues that his craft fulfils a need of the society, the professor refuses to take him seriously.

The movie was not successful at the box office. This was the end of the team, and the four names never came together in the credits of a movie again.

The 'team': Masroor (first left), Sohail (second left), Waheed (second right) and Pervez (first right). Sitting in front of Waheed is c. Mandody.

---

[1] Obituary of Waheed Murad by Pervez Malik in Urdu, anthologized in S. A. Najam (Urdu; n.d.), pp.64-75

Zeba and Waheed in Beirut on location for *Rishta Hai Pyar Ka*

The success of *Armaan* brought tremendous demand on Waheed to work as actor and he responded by becoming one of the busiest actors at that time. With the mental energy of a genius, he managed his hectic schedules without keeping a diary – and with unfailing punctuality. When asked by the journalist friend Asif Noorani how he remembered the dates, he pointed to his head and said that it was all there.[1]

In spite of becoming one of the busiest actors, he retained his interest in production and continued presenting a movie under his own banner every year until a year after the separation of East Pakistan: *Samandar* (1968), *Ishara* (1969), *Naseeb Apna Apna* (1970), *Mastana Mahi* (1971; Punjabi), *Jaal* (1972) and *Hero* (1985, released posthumously). The last two were in colour.

He was often called the chocolate-cream hero (and in Urdu, sometimes just 'the chocolate hero'). The title may have been inspired initially from the play *Arms and the Man* (1898) by George Bernard Shaw, where Raina Petkoff calls Captain Bluntschli her 'Chocolate Cream Soldier' because he carries chocolate instead of ammunition ('What use are cartridges in battle? I always carry chocolate instead.').[2]

---

[1] The author remembers reading this in an old issue of *Eastern Films* from the 1960s, but unfortunately the files of that magazine could not be accessed now.
[2] George Bernard Shaw (1898/1913), p.14. Modern criticism finds Bluntschli as a

Waheed kept wondering why the epithet was applied to him. 'Chocolate is dark, cream is white,' he said jokingly in a radio interview in the last year of his life, and added that his complexion was dusky but not dark enough to be compared to chocolate.[1] He was most commonly appreciated for his portrayal of romantic roles and the filming of love songs. Undoubtedly, he was the heartthrob of millions, although in his lifetime the predominance appeared to be rivaled by two powerful contenders – Muhammad Ali, who stole the Nigar for best actor from him in 1966, the year of *Armaan;* and Nadeem, who made his debut with the immensely popular *Chakori* in 1967.

Yet, no other celebrity of the cinema could boast of having as deep an impact on people from such diverse social strata as Waheed. Iqbal Mahdi, a celebrated painter of the times, was reported to have watched *Mastana Mahi* repeatedly for several days. Raju Jamil, the son of the great poet Jamiluddi Aali, watched many of the movies of Waheed more than a dozen times each, and proudly copied the distinct hair style of the star. 'I almost went in trance when I met Waheed Murad the first time ever,' he recalls about his visit to the sets of *Armaan* in the Eastern Studios, courtesy his family friend Sohail Rana.[2]

On the other end of the social spectrum, people in the low-income locality, Layari, in Karachi, have continued to hail him as their collective alter-ego, beginning with his portrayal of a donkey-cart driver in *Heera Aur Pather* (which is sometimes called the 'national film' of the Layari community).[3]

The founder of his first fan club, Fareed Ashraf Ghazi, was the grandson of Maulana Muhammad Shafi, the first grand mufti of Pakistan. Other fan clubs followed, and new ones have kept coming up ever since, often led by people who may not have been interested in movies otherwise.

---

hero to be 'a bit lightweight, and his "chocolate cream soldier" romance with Raina a bit sentimental'. See Christopher Innes, Ed. (1998/2004), p.135

[1] The interview was taken by Khushbakht Shujaat in 1983. I remember the conversation from a recording which I once had but do not have it.

[2] Raju Jamil (2008)

[3] Raju Jamil (2008)

His firstborn, Aalia, was born in Karachi on December 23, 1969. Waheed was overjoyed and when he went to visit Salma in the hospital, he asked the nurse, 'Where is my heroine?' The nurse thought that he was asking about Salma and answered accordingly but he corrected her by saying, 'No, I mean the little one.'[1]

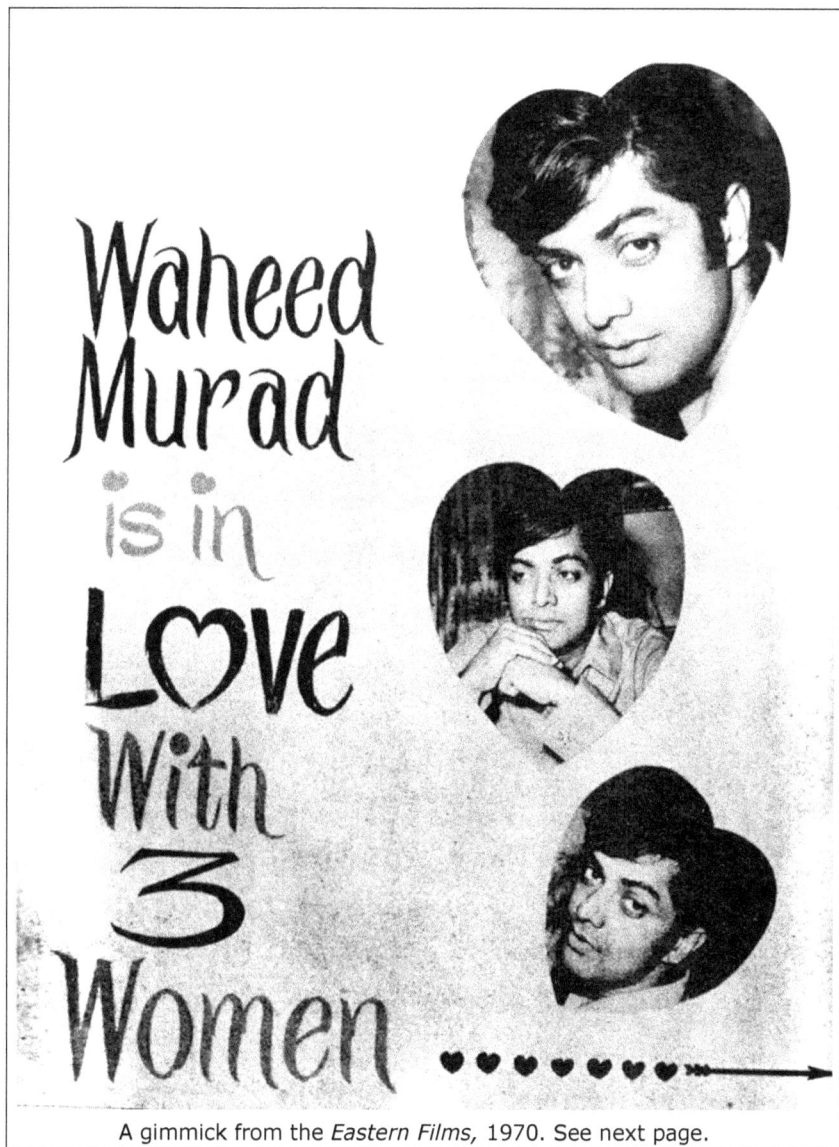

A gimmick from the *Eastern Films,* 1970. See next page.

---

[1] Reported to the author by Mrs. Salma Murad

45

Y E S------ I am in love with three women and they all live in the same house.

Shireen Murad

The first is a married woman; fortunately she is married to my father and since she is my mother there are no complications.

Anytime I think of whatever little I have achieved I cannot do so without thinking that it was her love and affection, her care and guidance, her thoughtfulness and encouragement when I most needed it, that made everything possible for me. Everything I am, all I have I would lay at her feet and still feel I have done nothing.

Salma Murad

The second is Salma, also married, but to me and of her own choice. For her courage I admire her. She opted to share my home and my name, happiness and sorrows, good times and bad. Hers is a major gamble and for her sake I hope I prove worthy.

Aliya Murad

And now the third. My daughter Aalia, six months old and already she has wrapped me around her little finger. At the same time the tyrant and darling of the house, she does not ask, she commands and whatever Aalia wants Aalia gets. Once she is contented she will reward me with a smile and its ample compensation. For more than anything in life I want to see Aalia smiling............... always!

Waheed Murad

EASTERN FILM

A page from *Eastern Films,* published some time in 1970.

Six months later, he was writing about her in a magazine: '... already she has wrapped me around her little finger. At the same time the tyrant and darling of the house, she does not ask, she commands and whatever Aalia wants Aalia gets. Once she is contented she will reward me with a smile and it's simple compensation. For more than anything in life I want to see Aalia smiling ... always!' (See facsimile on the facing page).

Saadia, a second daughter, was also born in Karachi but died in less than two months, leaving her parents grief-stricken.

The third was a son, Adil, born in Lahore on November 13, 1976.

On the outdoor shoots within the country, Waheed was usually accompanied by Salma ('Bibi' as he called her endearingly) – and later by Aalia too. For shooting abroad he usually had to go alone.

The letters he wrote to Salma during one such trip – from Japan where he went for the shoot of *Khamosh Nigahain* – are fortunately well-preserved, providing some rare glimpses into his family life in his own words. They are being produced here in their entirety.

5th July 70.[1]

My darling,

There was a quick change in programme and so we skipped Manilla [*sic.* Manila] for the time being and came to Tokyo – long 8 hrs. flight – got here at midnight – but WOW – this place is just fabulous – makes every city we have ever seen look like a village – it's modern, it's clean, it's huge,[2] the people are friendly and everything is so expensive you feel like screaming. There was no accommodation anywhere except here which is one of the 3 or 4 most expensive & lovely hotels of Tokyo – too bad for the producer but thank God he is bighearted about it all – his further bad luck is that the weather is completely foul and no one has seen the sun here in the last three weeks. Pray for us – we have such a lot of work to do.

Today we spent in the Ginza – one big area with fabulous stores and the night life of the city. It needs a lot of will power to not go crazy – I think one could spend all one's [through?] in one hour in one store.

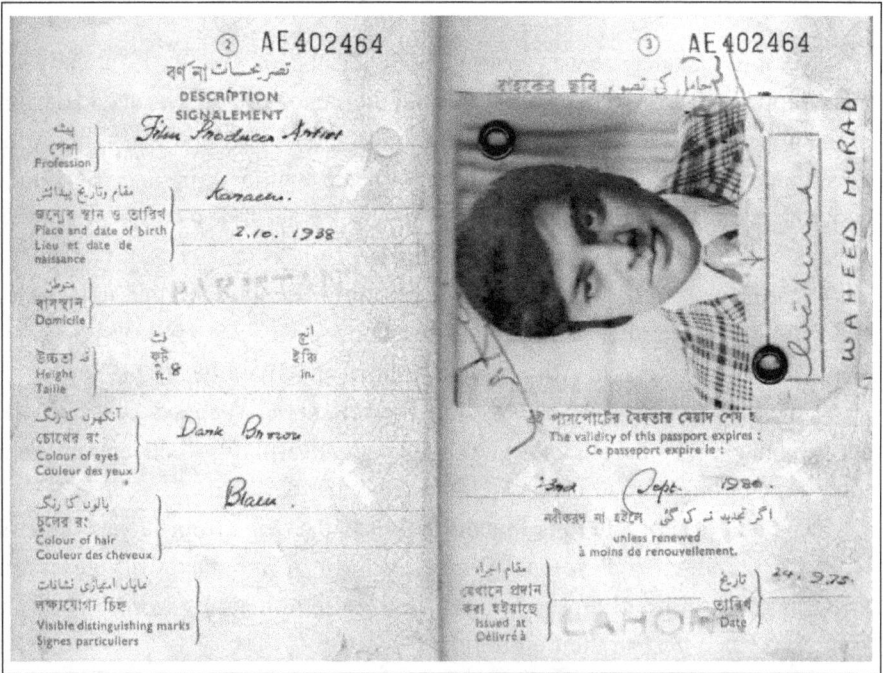

---

[1] Letterhead: Hotel The New Otani Tokyo. Tel. (03) 265-1111 Cable Address: Hotel Newtani Tokyo.

[2] Waheed wrote it as 'its modern, its clean, its huge'.

Everything is superb, but the TOYS – oh my love the toys are lovely – I feel like bringing home a planeful for my Bacha.

Daddy's telegram to me in Bangkok was vague but reassuring – it said Aalia was perfectly alright and you were improving & of all things that's exactly what I wanted to hear, – exactly what it needs to make me feel well again. We will be at this address for the next 4 days after which we will probably shift to another hotel nearer the locations we need & then to Osaka. I may have to send my regards to Issa if things get out of hand in which case I will give you a telegram. I'm anxious about Mummy, I wouldn't write her but I don't know if she is still in London or not. Anyway if Dad calls her or you write send her my love.

Use my car a bit and bring it up to 1000 miles – then the driver can take it for the 2nd servicing [&] after that we can to Sehwan & really test that buggy.

My regards to Daddy – All my love to Aalia – and to you, all of me forever. Yours
Waheed

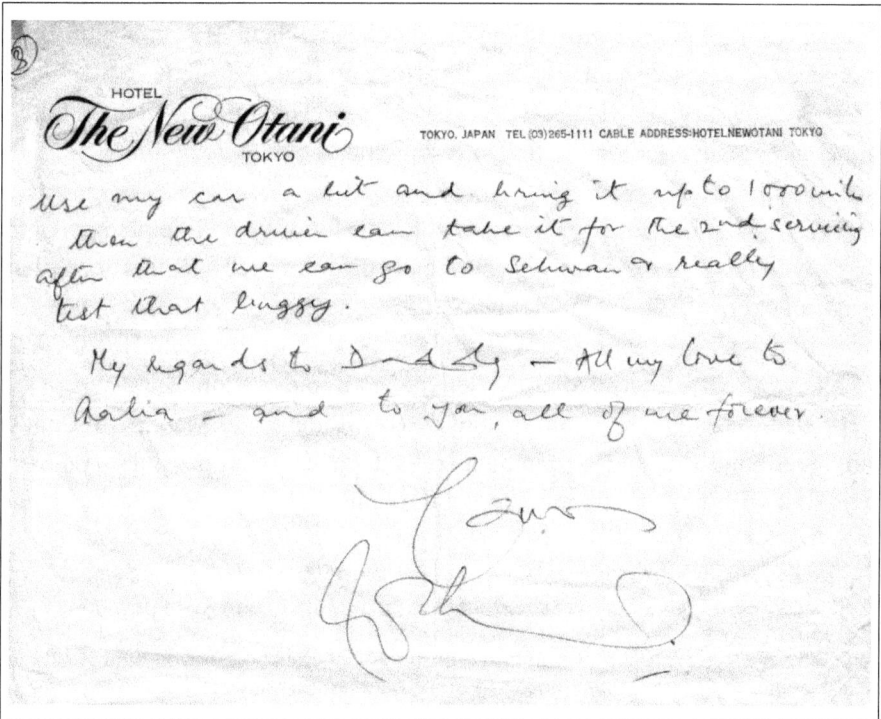

7th July 70[1]

Dearest,

Dad's telegram came and told me nothing. I'm waiting for a letter from you. Meanwhile a thousand times a day my thoughts drift home.

Tokyo is all sorts of things but we are not getting much work done. There's a constant sickening drizzle. All we could do was part of a song by night in Ginza – Ginza all lit up at night is a sight to behold.[2]

Seen the shopping around here – but most of the local people & some Pakistanis from the P.I.A. also suggest waiting till Hongkong[3] [Hong Kong]. I believe most things are far cheaper there. Rozina's mother has however gone mad; she has to be dragged away from the shops.

We are starving – the food everywhere is God damned awful. Spent much time and money looking for Indian restaurants. Found two and they were the worst of the lot.

I've[4] bought a super camera – will have a lot of fun taking pictures of the baby with this – its exposing is so perfect – you don't need sunguns or anything – it will expose even by candlelight.

I think as an economy move we might be shifting to Daichi Hotel, Ginza, in a day or two – if write after this letter send it to this address.

Dad said in his telegram that all of you at home and Mamma in London are well. Kindly all of [you] remain so – and as happy as possible – knowing this so it will [be] easier for me to get through.

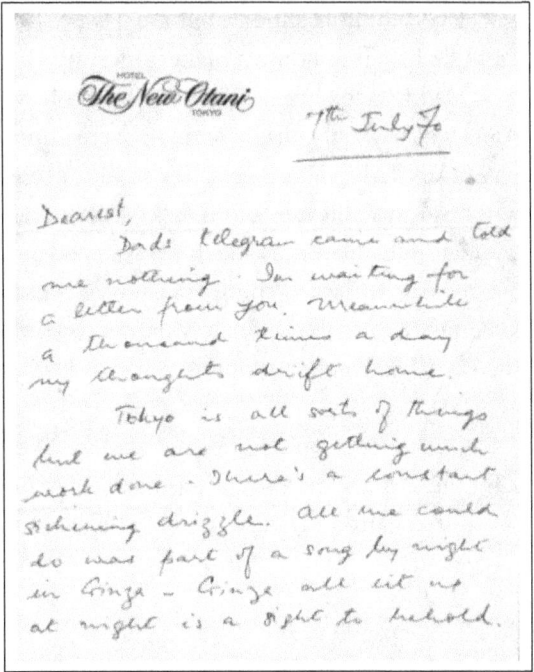

---

[1] Hotel Newtani Tokyo.
[2] The song may have been 'Lakhoan haseen hain mujhay tum kyun pasand ho'.
[3] The name was often written as a single word until the other form was adopted officially in 1926. The old form lingered on unofficially, retained even by institutions like Hongkong Post and the Hongkong and Shanghai Banking Corporation.
[4] Waheed has written it as 'Ive'.

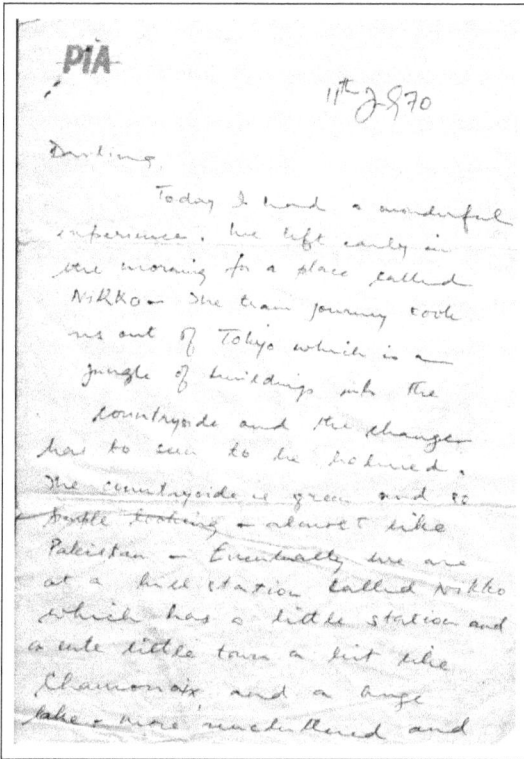

11th July 70[1]

Darling,

Today I had a wonderful experience. We left early in the morning for a place called Nikko – the train journey took us out of Tokyo which is a jungle of buildings into the countryside and the change has to [be] seen to be believed. The countryside is green and so simple looking – almost like Pakistan – Eventually we are at a hill station called Nikko which has a little station and a cute little town a bit like Chamonix[2], and a huge lake – more uncluttered and serene than the lakes in Geneva. And then there was the waterfall a huge, high torrent which roared so loud we couldn't hear ourselves speak – we started a song there[3] but after a while such thick fog came down that the taxi literally crawled back to the station. Not much work done but a day made pleasant & satisfying by the sheer beauty of the place.

Tomorrow morning we leave for Osaka – a most unnerving venture – we have no surety about our hotel reservations or anything. My mail from here will be forwarded so drop me a line to tell me how you and Aalia are.

I constantly think that this trip to Japan is only for the purpose of checking up and gathering information – a scouting expedition – the expedition proper will come when you & I and Aalia visit here soon. – I have fallen in love with Japan – And I love you and I love Aalia and God bless you both.

Waheed

---

[1] Letterhead: PIA
[2] Chamonix Mont-Blanc is one of the oldest ski resorts in France, about 70 miles from Lake Geneva.
[3] This must have been the song 'Kabhi tou maango'

OTTTTTTI1

ZCZC JCP449 KAR LAH38, PWKX CO JPOS 016,

OSAKA 16/15 19 2113

SALMA MURAD C/0 VARIETY KARACHI

CABLE RECEIVED GODBLESS YOU AND AALIA MY WORLD IS COMPLETE

WAHEED

Osaka[1]

20th July 70

Darling,

I finally got a letter – redirected Daichi Tokyo – Everybody in the unit has been having the same trouble with their mail – the first letters we received were yours & one for Munawar Zarif – And everyone one was thrilled as if Santa Claus had come.

I'm in bed with – flu – All of sudden I had high fever & a sore throat & all kinds of aches & pains – wouldn't get up for 2 days – thank God we had finished the bulk of shooting at the Expo.

Tomorrow I'll be up to finish what is left. On the 23rd we should go to Tokyo – there is a couple of days work in Toyo – the unit will stay on to finish their Punjabi thing – I'll go to Hongkong [Hong Kong] for 2 or 3 days & then to Bangkok or Manilla [sic. Manila] to get a PIA flight to Karachi, probably 28th or 29th.

It's been a long & tiring trip & I wanna go home. I won't be writing after this as I will probably be there before the letter and will cable you my detailed programme the moment I have it.

Big kiss for my baby.

Love you,

Yours

Waheed

---

[1] Letterhead: Hotel New Hankyu, Tel. (06) 372-5101 Osaka, Japan

Waheed moved to Lahore in 1973, after the decline of the film industry in Karachi. He bought the house, 72-G, Gulberg III (not far from the graveyard).[1] He named the house Qasr-i-Armaan. The reference to his trend setting movie was not without a pun, since the name of the house in Persian (and Urdu) could be translated as 'the Palace of Dreams'.

He did not produce any movie under his banner during the rest of the decade. Speaking to a film journalist soon after moving to Lahore, he said that he had several stories in his mind and was finding it difficult to choose.[2] The next year, in 1974, he appeared in as many as 13 movies, three of which celebrated a Golden Jubilee. In 1976, again he appeared in 13 movies. By then he had also become popular in Punjabi movies. That year, *Shabana* became his first movie to celebrate a Diamond Jubilee (cumulative run of 100 weeks). Till the end of the decade he seemed to be busier than ever before, but many of these movies featured more than one male actor in lead roles, and sometime as many as three – for instance, Waheed, Muhammad Ali and Nadeem together in *Shama*. Frequently, he was teamed up with Shahid, the new star who had appeared recently and had risen to fame.

It did not mean that most of his movies in the 1970s were second-grade productions, either because they were presented by less famous filmmakers or because the female lead was not a top-ranking heroine. Apparently, this impression was created due to speculations in the press about his fallout with various producers and heroines. Even if some of these speculations were true, working with a less famous filmmaker or a small-time heroine was nothing new for him. Like most of the other stars of those days, he had been accepting low-budget movies along with high-budget ones from the very beginning.[3] It remained the same in the 1970s. If some of the top-ranking producers, directors or heroines were not teamed with him at one time or another, others were. Big

---

[1] The address appears on his passport, cited in References.
[2] Shaukat Dar (Urdu; 1973)
[3] One famous exception to this common practice of those days was Nadeem, who worked in fewer movies and was said to charge a higher fee.

Seated L to R: Zarin Kamal, Salma Ahmad and Salma Murad. Standing L to R: film star Syed Kamal, cricketers Khalid Abdullah, Saeed Ahmad, another and Waheed.

projects continued to appear in his filmography along with smaller ones throughout the decade.

In retrospect it seems that the real problem that may have undermined his career – imperceptibly at the beginning – was an overall decline in creative imagination in Pakistan after the loss of its Eastern wing. In the case of movies, characters became more stereotypical and hence Waheed was cast more frequently in characters that aimed at selling the 'chocolate cream' side of his personality more than breaking new grounds.

Simply put, it was stagnation, and why it hit the mainstream culture of Pakistan so hard in the 1970s is another question altogether. What can be said on behalf of Waheed is that he did not take it passively, and without making an effort to fight back. Some of his assignments from this period were unmistakably experimental and different, such as *Naag Aur Nagin* and *Aurat Raj*. Some other assignments could reveal their originality through a deeper analysis, such as *Waqt, Wahda, Bahen Bhai* and *Parakh*. On his part, Waheed did not refrain even from playing an outright villain in *Sheeshey Ka Ghar*.

He was also experiencing setbacks on the personal front. Nisar Murad died in June 1982. It is possible that Waheed never recovered emotionally from the loss.

By this time, the Pakistani cinema had clearly passed its heyday – either because of the stagnation mentioned above, or due to other factors. At that time, the decline was usually blamed on the 'VCR'. Introduced in Pakistan in the mid-1970s, the video-cassette recorder remained an illegal item until 1984 but had already become part of the social fabric by 1980. The law-enforcing authorities simply looked the other way as VHS copies of Indian films were rented out illegally from shops in every neighbourhood. They offered an incomparably cheaper alternative to the cinema (renting a video cassette usually ranged from Rs. 10 to Rs. 20, whereas the price of a single cinema ticket could range from Rs.5 to Rs.15, depending on the category of seating).

The Indian film star Shatrughan Sinha (second from right), in a gathering in Lahore with the film producers Agha G. A. Gul and Shabab Keramvi on either side, and Waheed behind. The lady on the extreme left is the Pakistani film star Panna.

Perhaps it points to the symbolic significance of Waheed that the decline of the indigenous movie industry soon came to be discussed as 'the downfall of Waheed Murad'. Synchronicity would have it that these years were marked for him by health problems and their psychological accompaniments. He fell seriously ill in September 1980 and underwent surgery for appendicitis. He again fell ill in the summer of 1982, following the death of his father, and developed ulcer problems. On January 2, 1983, his ulcer burst and he was admitted to a private clinic in Lahore, where a part of his stomach was removed.

Incidentally, the Indian film star Amitabh Bachan had suffered from a stomach injury the same year, staying in coma for a week. Newspapers in Pakistan had also carried regular updates about his health, and now Waheed's surgery was compared with that incident in a write-up in the Urdu weekly *Akhbar-i-Jahan.* The press and the public were blamed for their lack of empathy towards the great living legend of their country.[1] The English weekly *Mag* ran a cover story about Waheed with the title 'What a Rise and...' It featured a detailed interview with him in which he reviewed the worsening condition of

On the sets of the TV show *Silver Jubilee:* actor-writer Athar Shah Khan, poet Parveen Shakir, Waheed, senior bureaucrat Mr. Nizami and Anwar Maqsood

---

[1] The article was written by the cartoonist Javid Iqbal and appeared in the Urdu weekly Akhbar-Jahan published by the Jang Media Group in 1982 or 1983.

the film industry and blamed it on a lack of education.[1] Appearing in the television show *Silver Jubilee* some time afterwards, he said that the film trade offered him little chance of putting his educational qualifications to good use: 'someone who has not even studied in Grade 1 has better chances of success here.' In the same interview he also revealed that he felt fed up with the erratic routine of his profession and was looking forward to change his career so that he may have a 9-to-5 routine and may get to spend his evenings with the family in a regular manner.[2] His appearance on television shocked people because he had lost so much weight.

In a radio interview a little later, he said, 'I think sometimes, when I will not be an actor anymore, or even if I am, but if something happens – I disappear suddenly, or I die – I would then like this song of mine to go on playing: "I am a tale forgotten, a thought that has passed; I am a question you failed to understand."' The song was from *Doraha*: '*Bhooli hui hoon dastaan, guzra hua khayal hoon; jiss to nah tum samajh sakay, mien aisa ik sawal hoon.*'[3]

This turned out to be his last interview. He had an accident while driving on Ravi Road, Lahore, in later September, 1983. The treatment left scars on his eyelid and lips, and plastic surgery was suggested.

He left for Karachi on November 11, with his son Adil. Salma and Aalia were in the United States, where they had gone for visiting Salma's sister Mariam Issa.

In Karachi, he still owned two apartments in the posh Sidco Centre Avenue, but stayed with his friend Col. Ayub, whose wife Mumtaz was like a

---

[1] The feature was compiled by the journalist Samarah Niazi. I had this issue of *Mag* in my personal collection for a very long time but unfortunately I do not have it now, and have not been able to access the files of *Mag*.
[2] The interview is cited in the References.
[3] The interview was taken by Khushbakht Shujaat in 1983. I remember the conversation from a recording which I once had but do not have anymore.

sister to him. There he celebrated the birthday of Adil on November 13, and the next day he booked an operation for plastic surgery at the Mid-East Clinic for November 24.

The operation never took place. In the early hours of November 23, Waheed suffered cardiac arrest and passed away. The body was taken to his mother in Lahore. Her grief was unbearable. She had lost her husband the previous year and now her only son was dead at the age of forty-five.

The news spread like a forest fire, and was

Waheed with his son Adil

received with shock bordering on disbelief. Film studios were closed down immediately, and colleagues rushed to Waheed's residence – Muhammad Ali did not even waste time in removing the makeup he was wearing for a shoot at that time. Multitudes of fans thronged to the funeral.

Pervez Malik was among the friends in charge of the funeral. As they were pushing back the crowds, one of the unknown fans looked at him and said, 'We loved Waheed Murad very much. Do we not have any right on him?' Pervez stepped back. Thereafter it was mainly the fans and followers of Waheed who lifted his coffin and lowered it into the grave, alongside his friends.[1]

Salma and Aalia arrived shortly afterwards. They had hurried back from the United States as soon as they received the news, but could not get a direct flight.

---

[1] Obituary of Waheed Murad by Pervez Malik in Urdu, anthologized in S. A. Najam (Urdu; n.d.), pp.64-75

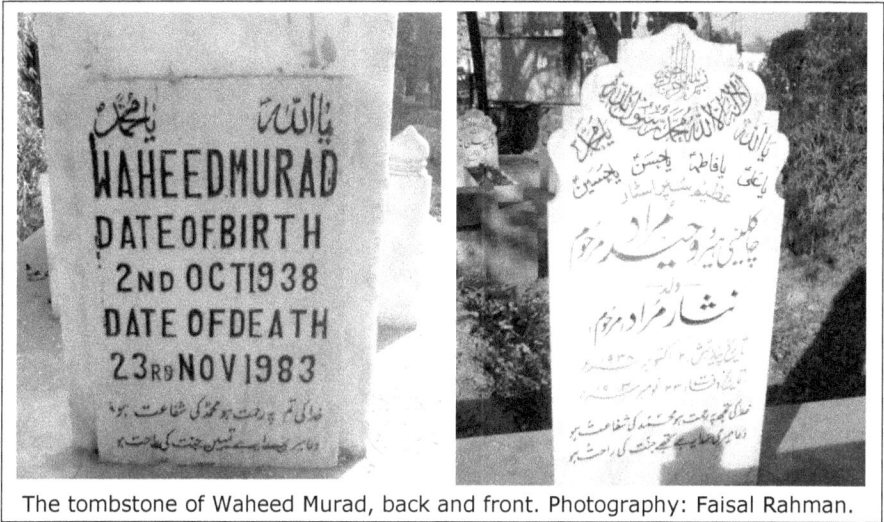

The tombstone of Waheed Murad, back and front. Photography: Faisal Rahman.

The next year, 1984, passed like a year of mourning. Almost the entire repertoire of his movies was brought back to cinemas, and the advertisements were usually written like obituaries.

In addition to special issues of magazines and newspapers, there were also books that came out with titles like *Who Killed Waheed Murad? (Waheed Murad Ka Qatil Kaun?)*. Special audio cassettes of his songs came out with passionate commentaries that could move many listeners to tears, and they often did. In those days, it may have been difficult to walk across a city centre in Pakistan without hearing a song of Waheed, or one of those audio-recorded obituaries.

In cinemas where his old movies were re-released, his fans provided commemorative posters and decorated the foyers with more 'fanfare' than premieres of new movies were getting at that time. In those foyers, people wept without feeling embarrassed about it. Strangers from diverse social backgrounds were seen sharing their feelings about the dead artist unreservedly.

Thirteen months of mourning ended with the posthumous release of Waheed's last production, *Hero,* on January 11, 1985. Tears were shed again, but a catharsis was also found – and a sense of relief that the movie, initially abandoned after his death, had finally been completed 'on popular demand'.

In the meanwhile, a cult had been born. His first death anniversary was observed by his fans with recitals of the Quran, and prayers for his soul. This has been happening across the country every year since then.

Waheed (centre) with Sohail Rana (left) and Pervez Malik (right)

Chapter 2
The Filmmaker

The recurring themes and motifs in the work of a filmmaker may reveal something about his or her personality and also reflect the the complex interaction between the filmmaker and his or her culture.[1]

It has been noticed, quite famously, that blondes are often subjected to various manners of degradation in the movies of Alfred Hitchcock: hand-cuffed to a man, slashed to death in a shower or having their faces pecked by ferocious birds, and so on.[2] The films of the Indian director Subhash Ghai have often been about strained relationship between friends or brothers, and an early childhood song highlights this thread in the storyline.[3]

In Pakistan, the movies of the director Fareed Ahmad were almost always about mistaken identity. Hassan Tariq typically relied on the love triangle. In his version of *Laila Majnu* – featuring Waheed as well – the role of the rival, the Iraqi prince, became much more emphasized than in the original Persian poem. There were two triangles in *Shama Aur Parvana* and *Naag Aur Nagin*, and even three in *Anjuman.* [4]

As a filmmaker, Waheed produced eleven movies. The first two may be excluded from the present study, since they were pilot projects undertaken

---

[1] Michael Walker (2005), p.18
[2] See, for example, Michael Walker (2005), p.83: 'From the attempted rape of Alice in *Blackmail* to the murder of Brenda in *Frenzy* blondes have been Hitchcock's most regular victims.' Instances cited in the text are from *Thirty-Nine Steps, Psycho* and *The Birds*.
[3] Khurram Ali Shafique 1995 (d)
[4] Khurram Ali Shafique 1995 (d).

Young Waheed with his senior family friend, Syed Musa Raza, better known as Santosh Kumar - the greatest Pakistani super star before Waheed.

while he was still a student. Of the other nine he may be regarded as the 'author'.[1]

'He took a personal interest in every department of film,' Pervez Malik later wrote. 'His opinion would be reflected in everything – story, music, set, wardrobe, and so on.'[2]

According to Sohail Rana, 'He was a complete film personality – producer, actor, director and writer.'[3]

The basic idea that inspired Waheed to turn to movies was described by his childhood friend Javid Ali Khan in the following words:

> We grew up with a mind to serve the nation just the way the Quaid-i-Azam and Quaid-i-Millat Liaquat Ali Khan had asked us to do. Waheed believed that he could do this through movies.[4]

The relevance of cultural activities such as filmmaking to the vision of the founding parents of Pakistan is one of the most neglected aspects of Pakistan's history and will be discussed further in the epilogue.

Here it may suffice to say that Waheed grew up in times when it was only natural to think about serving the nation. Given his environment, it was equally natural for him to think that he could do this through the medium of cinema.

A very good description of that environment has been given to us by Pervez Malik:

---

[1] Technically, the production house is considered to be the author of a movie. The term 'auteur' ('author' in French) has been deliberately avoided here because it is usually used for someone who projects his or her personal vision through a movie but so far it has not been applied to a visionary who may have discovered the true general will of the society in his or her conscience, which is the possibility being considered here.

[2] Obituary of Waheed Murad by Pervez Malik in Urdu, anthologized in S. A. Najam (Urdu; n.d.), pp.64-75

[3] Adeel A. Khan (2009)

[4] Reply of Javid Ali Khan to the author's specific question about the primary inspiration of Waheed Murad as an artist.

In this whole period [from childhood to youth], the home of Waheed was the centre of our social activities. Now the family of Waheed had moved to a large house [in P.E.C.H. Society], where some function was held every weekend and all of us got together for that. As such the circle of Waheed's friends was quite wide but his closest friends even now were his [former] schoolmates.

Waheed was very popular among girls even during his college days. Being the son of a wealthy father he used to wear the best clothes, drove his own car even to the college, and besides, he had immense self-confidence from the very beginning. He was [also] fond of music and dance, and was a dancer par excellence.

Since his father was a successful film distributor, there was an atmosphere of movies even at his home. Film celebrities were given receptions at his place on their visits to Karachi. All of us friends also attended such receptions, and it was here at the house of Waheed that I saw the famous film stars of those days, which included Santosh Kumar, Sabiha Khanum, Shamim Ara, Ala-ud-din, Talish and many others. Besides, whenever Nisar Murad took a film for distribution, he first arranged its viewing at his home, in which we all participated. Then it was discussed. We would all give our comments and make predictions about the success or failure of the film.

This was the atmosphere which evoked in me a passion for cinema, otherwise what did I, the son of an army officer, have to do with the film industry![1]

It is also interesting to note that Pervez, receiving inspiration from the environment at Waheed's home, turned out to be one of the most patriotic filmmakers. Most of the artists whom Waheed brought under his banner Film Arts were patriotic with a religious consciousness:

- The first two movies of Film Arts were directed by Munawar Rashid (pronounced 'Rasheed'), who got his break as a director with them. Rashid, whose son Haroon later became a famous cricketer, was known for keeping a strict discipline and eventually left the film trade for religious reasons.

---

[1] Obituary of Waheed Murad by Pervez Malik in Urdu, anthologized in S. A. Najam (Urdu; n.d.), pp.64-75

- Syed Iqbal Hussain Rizvi, who wrote the scripts of the first two movies of Film Arts, and later also of *Heera Aur Pather* and *Naseeb Apna Apna*, had 'participated' in the election of 1945-46 as a child of twelve by making a big flag of the All-India Muslim League and carrying it through the streets of Aligarh.
- Himayat Ali Shair, who wrote some of the lyrics for *Jabse Dekha Hai Tumhen*, was initially influenced by the Marxist-oriented 'Progressive Writers Association' but did not go all the way with it. He contributed an uplifting patriotic song for *Jabse Dekha Hai Tumhen*, and later gained special recognition for his groundbreaking research on the *naat* poetry (odes to the Prophet, peace be upon him).
- National songs by the poets Masroor Anwar and Sehba Akhtar, and set to music by Sohail Rana, have become the very substance with which successive generations have been creating a national consciousness.
- Among many other names associated with the banner of Film Arts, two cannot be skipped: the actor Azad, who had formerly been the driver of the Quaid-i-Azam; and Zahoor Ahmad, who later became known for his plays about the heroes of Muslim history and the issue of Kashmir (the title of his obituary in a leading newspaper was 'Adieu to a veteran and a patriot'[1]).

Patriotism is defined variously by various people. The individuals named here – with the possible exception of Himayat Ali Shair – took patriotism to mean that the guidelines left behind by the founding parents should be followed instead of turning to any other ideology, and that every citizen should work devotedly.[2]

In the inner circle of Waheed, and under his banner, one could not find individuals who were sceptical about the idea of Pakistan. Javid Ali Khan once introduced Waheed to the poet Faiz Ahmad Faiz, who at once recalled Waheed's grandfather from his Sialkot days. In spite of this very pleasant meeting, Waheed did not stay in touch with Faiz.[3]

---

[1] [Anonymous] (2009). See 'References' for details.
[2] These are the well-known views of the persons named here. To cite a few examples: for Pervez Malik, see Shafique (1996b); for Sohail Rana, see 'Inspiration message from Sohail Rana' cited among electronic sources in the References; detailed views on the subject expressed by Syed Iqbal Hussain Rizvi were recorded on audio during the author's interview with him.
[3] Narrated to the author by Javid Ali Khan.

Fatima Jinnah, the sister of the late Quaid-i-Azam, affectionately called the Madar-i-Millat or 'the Mother of the Nation', was nominated as the presidential candidate by a coalition of almost all political parties in late 1964. The election was to be held in early 1965.

The election campaign that took both wings of the country by storm involved a lot more than choosing a ruler. It was passionately debated whether the unschooled masses were entitled to free will as implied in the creation of Pakistan, or whether they were unfit for democracy as claimed by President Field Marshall General Ayub Khan. Using the latter argument as a pretext, Ayub had introduced a system of indirect election – 'Basic Democracy' as it was called – in which the masses only chose 80,000 electors who in turn chose the President.

Fatima Jinnah at the wedding reception of the sister of Salma Murad. L to R: Salma, Noor Jehan Maker (Salma's mother), Mariam Maker Issa, Fatima Jinnah

Madar-i-Millat stated boldly that Pakistan was brought into existence by the people 'through wise and fearless exercise of their franchise' and it was therefore 'an irony of history' that the same people should 'today be asking for enfranchisement'.[1] She asked 'whether the people of Pakistan who exercised direct vote before independence have suddenly undergone a metamorphosis which has incapacitated them from exercising their vote in like manner now.'[2]

The debate preoccupied the nation throughout the months of October, November and December, and was still going on when *Heera Aur Pather* was released on December 11, 1964.

The theme had occurred to Waheed some time earlier during a trip to Dacca [now Dhaka], the provincial capital of East Pakistan at that time.[3] The script was developed by Iqbal Hussain Rizvi, and initially Waheed had also agreed to let him direct the movie since Munawar had become too busy with assignments in Lahore. Masroor wrote five out of the eight songs while three were penned by another emerging poet Mauj Lakhnavi. Sohail composed the soundtrack as usual.

Some time afterwards, Rizvi backed out of the project. In his words:

Sometimes one overestimates things in the process of directing a movie, and even overestimates friendship. There were some tensions in the unit, and one day I got carried away. I said [to Waheed], 'Leave it, friend. I won't direct your film.' And I left the project. The decision caused me a great setback but I shall not say that Waheed Murad was unfair to me by any means. He was a wonderful person. I am the one who backed out.[4]

In the meanwhile, Pervez Malik had returned with his degree in filmmaking from the UCLA. Initially, Waheed was not sure how far an education received abroad could be useful in the Pakistani context, and had asked Pervez to hang around for a while and study the local style of production. After the fallout with Rizvi, he asked Pervez to take up the megaphone. Since the film had already been well-conceived by then, Pervez could not change much except adding a few sequences, altering some others and asking Masroor to write additional dialogue for these new scenes. This was Masroor's break into writing dialogue.[5]

[1] Fatima Jinnah (1976), p.322
[2] Fatima Jinnah (1976), p.331
[3] Reported to the author by Syed Iqbal Hussain Rizvi
[4] Reported to the author by Syed Iqbal Hussain Rizvi

The subject of the movie bore resemblance to the political controversy of the day, even if unintended by its creators, and unnoticed by the viewers at that time. Still, the allegorical element was present in the very title of the movie. Literally, it meant 'the gem and the stone', and referred to two brothers in the story.

Hameed (Ibrahim Nafis) and Janu (Waheed Murad) are sons of a poor labour, Khairu (Kamal Irani), who can educate only one of his sons, so he chooses the elder one, Hameed. After completing his education in the nearby city, Hameed fears unemployment and marries Salma, the daughter of a wealthy industrialist (Agha Jan). In order to hide his humble background, he says that he has no relatives. Thereafter, he cannot disclose his relationship with his father, brother or sister – Zebo (Nimmi) – when they need him. He watches silently while they suffer abuses from his arrogant and villainous brother-in-law Sajid (Adeeb). When the truth is revealed, Hameed is admonished even by his father-in-law, who says that it is no shame to be born poor.

This was a rebuttal of the idea that the unschooled masses should not be involved in decision-making.[1] The well-educated Hameed, whom his father had treated as a 'gem' turned out to be a worthless 'stone', and the unschooled Janu, considered worthless due to his lack of education, proved to be better. If Pakistan could be seen as a family – as S. M. Yusuf had recently suggested in the blockbuster *Ashiana* – should its affairs be decided by Hameed, or by Janu?

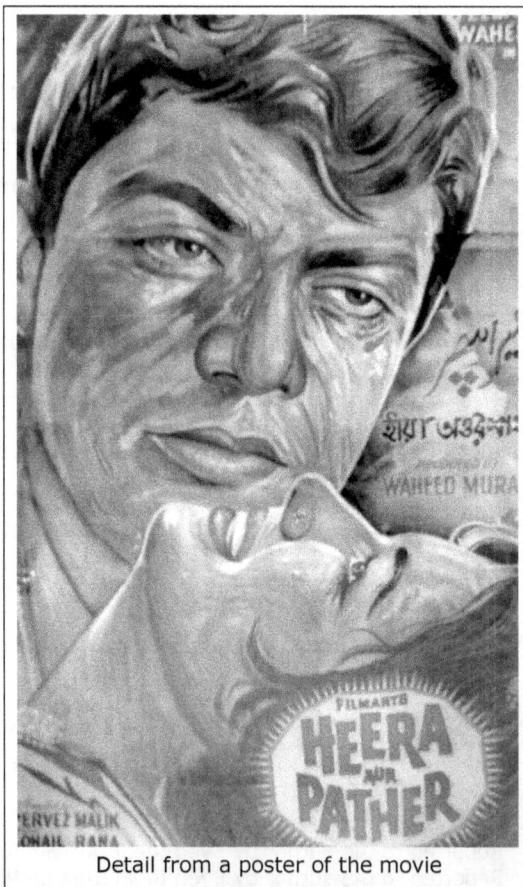
Detail from a poster of the movie

[5] Shafique (1996b)
[1] This observation was corroborated by Iqbal Rizvi, the screenwriter of the movie, in his meeting with the present author cited in the 'References'.

Waheed and Zeba as Janu and Nuri in *Heera Aur Pather*

In that fateful December of 1964, some of the educated cinemagoers may have unconsciously identified themselves with Hameed. Just like him, they had bartered self-respect for job security. They had watched the President and his cronies reviling the Mother of the Nation, just as Hameed watched Sajid slap his old father in the movie.

That the movie has remained popular among the politically agile residents of Layari in Karachi may not be just because the protagonist drives a donkey cart like some of them. Unlike both capitalism and socialism, *Heera Aur Pather* links the idea of social justice with the ethical concept of brotherly love. 'This was deliberate because I am extremely religious, at least in my consciousness,' says Rizvi.[1]

[1] Reported to the author by Iqbal Rizvi

Juxtaposition of Pakistan over the house in S. M. Yusuf's *Ashiana*

The Mother of the Nation lost the presidential election, held on January 2, 1965. The general impression was that the election had been rigged by the ruling junta.

The spirit of unity, which the old lady had successfully inspired, came in handy when the nation faced a direct threat to its existence later that year. On September 6, Indian troops crossed the international boundary and advanced towards Lahore, Sialkot and Sargodha – with the largest number of tanks deployed in any battle since World War II.

Historians were going to dispute the causes, events and the aftermath of the war but it could be safely conceded that the people displayed a common determination for playing their part in the defence of their country.

Consequently, the peace agreement signed between Ayub and the Indian Prime Minister Lal Bahadur Shastri in Tashkent (Russia) on January 10, 1966, was resented in Pakistan because, in common perception, it appeared as if a war won on the battlefront had been lost on the negotiation table. On behalf of East Pakistan, which comprised the majority of the population, Sheikh Mujibur Rahman proposed 'Six Points' aimed at increasing provincial autonomy.

This was the backdrop against which *Armaan* (or *Aspiration*) was released on Friday, March 18, 1966, and instantly fired the imagination of the nation like no other movie had ever done before – as described at length in the previous chapter.

The genesis of *Armaan* could be traced back to a night in 1963 when Sohail heard a tune in his dream. It was a variation on the raga Aiman. He noted it down in the morning, giving it the dummy lines, '*Akele na jana hamein chhor kar tum. Tumharay bina hum bhala kiya jiyein gay.*'[1]

Initially, he sold it to a film producer but took it back when the producer refused to get it recorded in Lahore with a large orchestra of 65 musicians. He then kept it aside for his own production, which he was planning to launch with

---

[1] Reported to the author by Sohail Rana; partially mentioned in Shafique (1996a).

70

Waheed and Agha Sarwar in *Armaan*

Pervez by the title *Doraha*. One day, the tune reached the ear of Waheed while Sohail was humming it. '*Doraha* is a long way away,' Waheed said to him. 'I am launching my next film. I have even conceived the story and this song fits in well. The film is going to be called *Armaan*.'[1]

Waheed also agreed to get the song recorded in Lahore with an orchestra of 65 musicians in addition to two other conditions which Sohail placed before him. The song would appear in three versions, respectively a soft version in male voice, a mellow version in female voice with minimum accompaniments and a final version in female voice with full orchestra. Also, the last version must be the end of the entire movie, which should not have even a single frame beyond this song.[2]

By this time, a remarkable synergy had developed between Waheed, Pervez, Sohail and Masroor.

'I will not say we influenced one another. *We were one.*' Sohail said many years later. 'We use to spend a lot of time together. Even on the sets we remained friends. Waheed would never pretend to be vain or make us feel that he was the boss around there. We believed in respecting each other's work,

---

[1] Shafique (1996a).
[2] Reported to the author by Sohail Rana, and partially mentioned in Shafique (1996a). As quoted in Adeel A. Khan (2009), the female version of the song was composed keeping Madame Noor Jahan in mind, and Waheed also liked the choice, but due to a sheer coincidence they ended up without her, and the song was recorded with Mala instead.

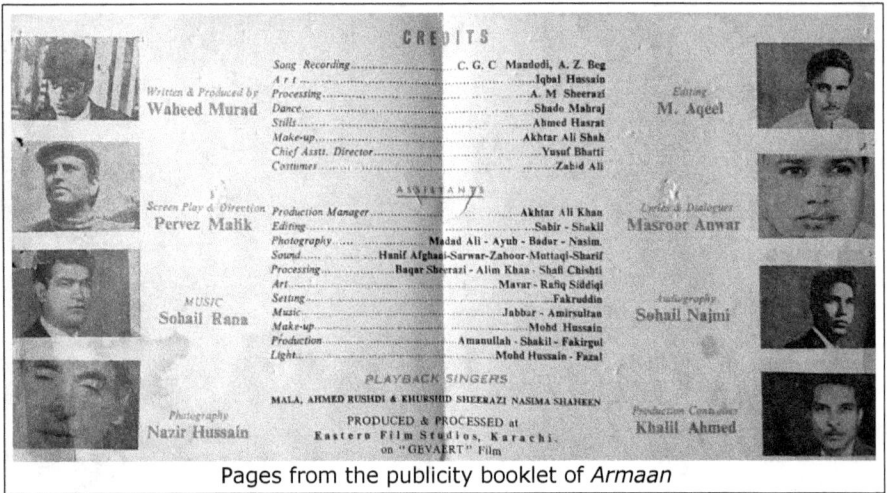

Pages from the publicity booklet of *Armaan*

feelings and efforts. And we never closed our minds to anybody's suggestion.'[1] According to Pervez, the song 'Akele na jana' became the anthem of their friendship:

> We used to sing it together in every party. Then Waheed and I wrote the script of *Armaan* keeping this song in front of us. When we came to Lahore for its recording, the four of us went together to the house of Mala [the singer] for singing it to her. All four of us started singing it together on harmonium ... On the first rehearsal of the song, tears rolled out of the eyes of all four of us.[2]

By saying that 'Waheed and I wrote the script of *Armaan,*' Pervez meant that the story was written by Waheed and the screenplay by him – as mentioned in the credits of the movie. Dialogue and lyrics were penned by Masroor Anwar.

Meanwhile, both Masroor and Sohail had gained the experience of stirring up the nation with their songs during the 1965 War. The remaining songs of *Armaan* were written soon afterwards.[3]

---

[1] Shafique (1996b)
[2] Obituary of Waheed Murad by Pervez Malik in Urdu, anthologized in S. A. Najam (Urdu; n.d.), pp.64-75
[3] Email of Sohail Rana conveyed to the author on October 17, 2008

Waheed and Zeba in *Armaan*

The film was conceived as a modern-day Cinderella story. The protagonist, Najma (Zeba), is an orphaned girl who lives in the beautiful hills of Murree with an unkind aunt (Bibbo) and two frivolous cousins, Dolly (Rozina) and Seema (Tarranum). The later has been away in a hostel in Lahore for completing her studies, and reveals to Najma that she had conceived a child from her lover Sohail, who has gone abroad for pursuing a bright career. Najma offers to keep her secret and raise the child anonymously. The aunt finds out and not knowing that the real mother of the child is Seema, she uses this against Najma just when Nasir (Waheed Murad), the wealthy but kind-hearted son of a family friend (Zahoor Ahmad) is about to take Najma as wife. The misunderstanding breaks the heart of Nasir and leads to a story where *Jane Eyre* meets *Wuthering Heights*, Seema gets married to Nasir but is eventually exposed when destiny runs it own course, Najma is presumed dead but returns just in time to stop Nasir for throwing himself off a cliff. The moral thrust of the story, according to Sohail, was on the gradual development of Nasir's character.[1]

Camera work, imagery and the use of symbolism were on a par with the best masterpieces of that time. Apart from the fact that the movie had to face a comparatively reduced competition because screening of the Indian movies had been banned since the recent war, the unprecedented response from the people could also indicate an unconscious desire for a charismatic leader who

---

[1] Shafique (1996a)

73

may uplift the masses and be transformed in the process. These were the kind of expectations people began to have of their leaders around this time. This was the year when Sheikh Mujib gained popularity in East Pakistan. In West Pakistan, the former Foreign Minister Zulfikar Ali Bhutto received an overwhelming welcome at Lahore Railway Station while passing through that city.[1]

The poster of *Armaan*

As mentioned earlier, *Armaan* turned out to be the first Pakistani Urdu film to celebrate a Platinum Jubilee. In addition to bagging awards for Waheed, Zeba, Mala and Ahmed Rushdi, it also brought a change in the trends as it pulled middle class families to the cinema.

The legend has proved to be enduring. In *Aina* (1977), the greatest movie of the director Nazrul Islam, the heroine was named Najma – possibly after the heroine of *Armaan*. In *Nahin Abhi Nahin* (1980), another movie of Nazrul, the main character was called Armaan. Nazrul even persuaded the actor playing the role, Faisal Rehman, to use Armaan as his screen name. Faisal himself grew up to conceive and direct a television sequel where a grown-up Armaan meets the spirit of Iqbal for learning about the existence and destiny of Pakistan. Officially produced by Iqbal Academy Pakistan, it was titled *Iqbal: an Approach to Pakistan* (Urdu; 2006). The script was written by the present writer, who had earlier written a made-for-TV film, *Socha Thha Pyar Na Karainge* (2001), inspired by the comedy sequences of *Armaan* and intended as a tribute to the classic. In 2012, another television channel produced a remake of *Armaan*, although it did not follow the original faithfully.

---

[1] The overall mood of the time, as reflected in Bhutto's own words, written a little later, was: 'A new look arid a new style will have to emerge. The old ways will no longer appeal to the people. It is no longer sufficient to be a fluent parliamentarian and an expert in repartee and to know when to make "a point of order", or to heckle and hound. A new all-round approach will have to be found in every facet of politics. The hand must reach the ground, the eye must perceive the sub-surface movements and the ear be able to hear the sound of music in the far distance.' Zulfikar Ali Bhutto (*n.d.*), p.36

The next production of Film Arts, *Ehsaan,* was released on June 30, 1967. This time, Masroor wrote the complete script – story, dialogue and lyrics. Apparently to break away from the sweeping romance of the previous venture, Zeba was presented as a widowed mother of a girl child and Waheed as a psychiatrist. His character, Aamir, was shown as an orphan brought up by a generous noble (Azad). Inspired by the example of the Prophet (peace be upon him), who had married a widow, Aamir chooses Saira (Zeba). He faces a dilemma when Saira's husband, Ashraf (Ibrahim Nafis), long presumed dead, returns as an amnesia patient. Performing his duty as if he was in the presence of God, Aamir treats him and revives his memory at the risk of losing Saira. It turns out that Ashraf was a monster so that Saira does not want to go back to him. Even the little daughter Zeb (Baby Jugnu) chooses Aamir over her father because Aamir has been more loving. Thematically, then, *Ehsaan* and the two previous movies could be taken together as a trilogy about the significance of God-consciousness in human relations.

Detail from the poster of the *Ehsaan*

In a way, the story came true for Zeba. Just as her character in the film discovered a caring husband who proved a good foster father to her daughter, Zeba found in the film star Muhammad Ali a worthy soul mate. They married on September 29, 1966, when, according to the journalist Asif Noorani, *Ehsaan* was about to go into production.[1] Just like Aamir in the movie, Ali adopted the daughter of Zeba from her first husband as his very own.

Clockwise from top: Waheed as Dr. Aamir; Azad as Nawab Sahib; Zeba as Saira, Waheed and Baby Jugnoo in *Ehsaan*.

---

[1] Asif Noorani (n.d.). The date of marriage is taken from Mazhar Iqbal (Website listed in 'References')

On January 6, 1968, the government of President Ayub Khan announced that a conspiracy had been uncovered between some personnel from East Pakistan and Indian politicians for establishing an independent state of Bangladesh. Twelve days later, Sheikh Mujibur Rehman was also implicated. He had already been under arrest for on account of his Six Points, presented in March 1966.

'The young Bengalis were quieter than usual at the Dacca and Chittagong Clubs,' the American Consulate General in Dhaka wrote secretly to the US Department of State a little later. 'Eid was quieter this year. Fear was in the air. Men were afraid to pass more than the barest of greetings. Once argumentative chaps endured the taunts of Punjabi and non-Bengali members.'[1]

This was the backdrop against which *Samandar,* the next venture of Film Arts, was released on March 10, 1968. Waheed had gathered a new team. The script was written by Agha Nazir Kawish and lyrics by Sehba Akhtar. Music was composed by Deebu Bhattacharya. Director was Rafiq Razvi, best known for his patriotic movie, *Bedari* (1957) – copied unabashedly from the Indian *Jagriti* (1954) but fulfilling an urgent need at the time of its release and making an enduring contribution with national songs like 'Ae Quaid-i-Azam tera ehsaan hai ehsaan'.

The female lead opposite Waheed was Shabnam, the brilliant talent from East Pakistan in her first role in a West Pakistani production. Since the two wings of the country were connected by the sea, and not by the land, the title song could also be interpreted symbolically: 'Saathi, tera mera saathi hai lehrata samandar' (Friend, the sea is our common friend).

The story was set in a fishing colony. Rajah (Waheed Murad) desires nothing except love. His best friend Jeera (Hanif) aspires to become the next chief of the community but ends up playing into the hands of Jaggu Seth (Rashid), a foreign intruder who wants to monopolise the economy. Rajah is persuaded by the people to contest a boat race through which the next chief would be elected. Rajah wins the race, but hands over the power to his former

---

[1] Shafique (2010c)

77

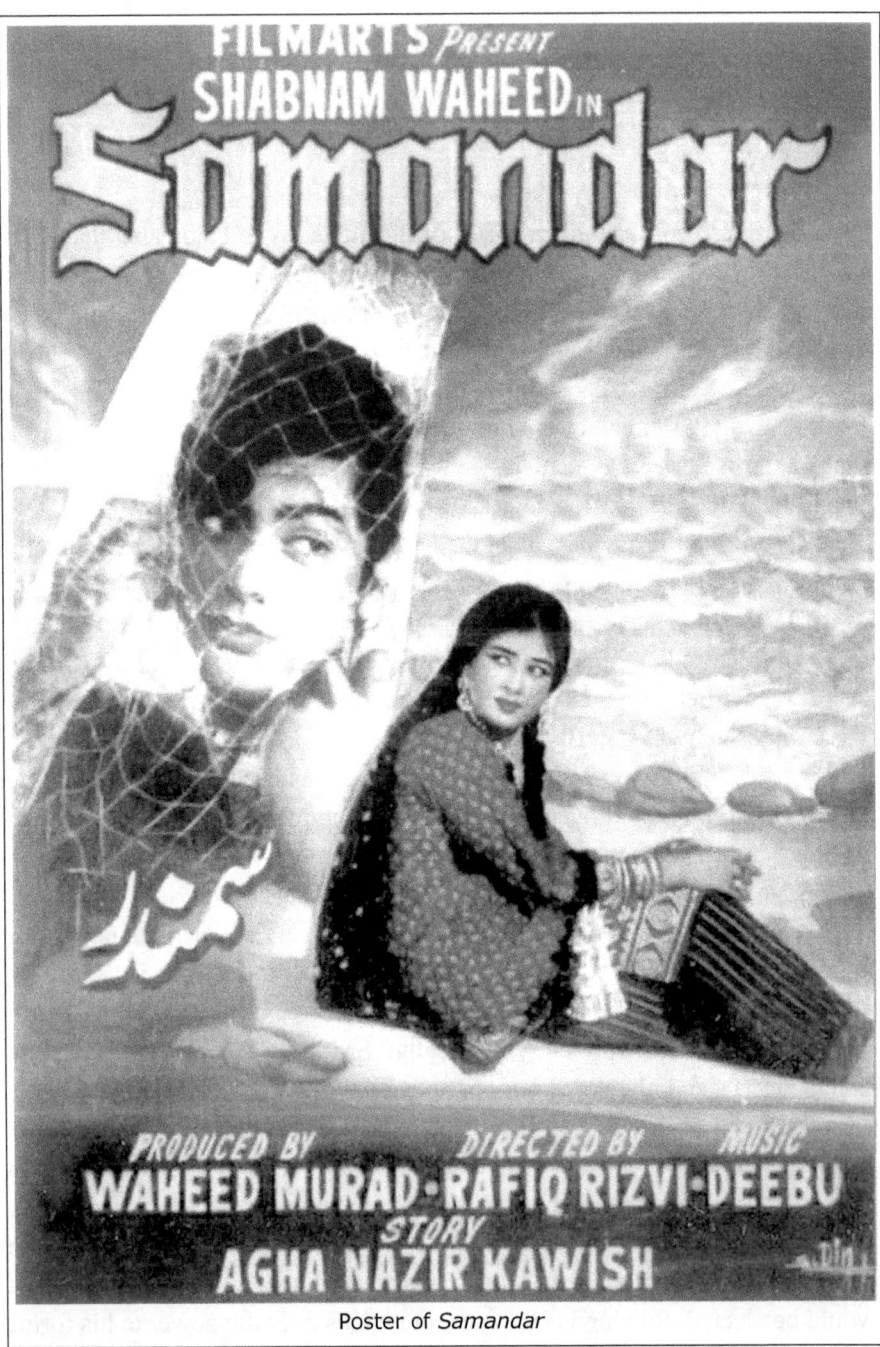

Poster of *Samandar*

friend after eliciting from him a promise that he would defend the community against the intruder.

If Jeera were to be taken as a symbolic representation of the politicians of East Pakistan, Rajah could be seen as an example of how the leaders of the Western wing should act. His love interest is Nuri (Shabnam), the chief's daughter, whom the custom requires to marry the next chief. As a symbol for the land and culture of East Pakistan, she was balanced out by Rajah's sister Bali (Rozina), who is wooed by Jeera. The paradox was that Rajah did not want to rule but still wanted to marry Nuri. This was not unlike the challenge the politicians of West Pakistan faced at that time: they were supposed to keep the federation together by the spiritual force of love and not by the physical force of imperialism.

The ailing chief of the community was depicted as unfit for the task as he admitted painfully, 'Old age, sickness and alcohol have rendered me incapable of taking a firm stance (against the enemy).' A community ruled by an inebriated head, threatened by foreign intrusion and divided against itself through mistrust, while fear lurked in the hearts of those whose love was pure – could there have been a more candid depiction of Pakistan in the hour of its existential crisis?

Rajah resolved the moral dilemma at the tomb of a local saint where the visitors were dressed to represent diverse ethnicities but the two singers rendering the traditional Sufi song addressed to Lal Shahbaz Qalandar wore Jinnah caps: spiritual ideals translated into political reality!

If carving a unified nation out of a diverse stock was to strive against the forces of nature[1], human beings appeared to be in conflict with nature in every song except the last, where it was announced that the lamps of the people have finally

Sehba Akhtar

---

[1] According to Iqbal, 'It is no exaggeration to say that Islam looks askance at Nature's race-building plans and creates, by means of its peculiar institutions, an outlook which would counteract the race building forces of nature.' See Iqbal (1977/1995), p.236

Waheed, Rozina and Hanif as Rajah, Bali and Jeera in *Samandar*

outshone the stars, and their garden boasts of a perfume that cannot be produced by Spring.

The movie may also be considered a rebuttal to the Marxist propaganda film, *Jago Hua Savera* (1959; promoted in English as *The Day Shall Dawn*). Conceived by the team of Faiz Ahmad Faiz from West Pakistan, the earlier movie was shot in East Pakistan. It presented a colony of fishers as the backdrop for a story that was an allegory about economic exploitation according to the Marxist worldview.[1] Some of the same motifs were used in *Samandar* with a completely different ethical purpose.

In the climax of *Samandar,* Rajah is persuaded by the people to enter the contest for succession against his friend Jeera, since Jeera has become a tool in the hands of alien exploiters. Rajah wins the contest and then corners his estranged friend before the entire community until Jeera ends up saying that if he had become the chief, he would also have defended the people against the foreign transgressor, and would have done even more than that. On this, Rajah hands over the rule to him, saying, 'Friend, I have no ambition to rule. My happiness is in the fulfilment of your desire. All I want is that you should keep the sanctity of this trust.' It is not known if anybody thought about applying the moral of this movie to the national politics in those days but in retrospect one can wish that it had been applied.

---

[1] According to Mushtaq Gazdar (1997), p.78: 'It was the story of an East Pakistani fisherman who strives hard to build a boat, a symbol of livelihood and sustenance for his entire family. All-pervasive poverty, depravation, ill health and ignorance are the major obstacles he has inherited from his environment ... [the film] reflected the socialist ideology through the struggle of the proletariat, viz., the fisherman.'

The next production of Film Arts, *Ishara,* was released on February 14, 1969. It was written, produced and directed by Waheed Murad. Masroor and Sohail returned to give dialogue and lyrics, and music, respectively. Waheed Murad and Deeba also sang a song, although it was not credited. The movie ran for a little over 25 cumulative weeks (Silver Jubilee).

As mentioned in the previous chapter, Waheed wanted to employ the stream of consciousness narrative mode in a mainstream Pakistani movie. *Ishara* lends itself to be interpreted as such a movie. It begins with the subjective camera moving into a street, and a voiceover welcoming the viewer. It can be presumed that what is seen here is what passes through the stream of the viewer's inner thoughts and perceptions while he or she is watching the movie. This also makes the viewer the main character and the movie becomes a story about his or her exploration of a new world. The new world is the movie that the viewer has just entered.

A second character is introduced almost simultaneously. It is the welcoming voice, *'Mera naam Aamir hai...'* ('My name is Aamir...'). Soon the viewer is taken to the room where Aamir paints his pictures. He is Waheed in the role of an aspiring painter. Out of three little children from the neighbourhood who are watching him paint the picture, the first child likes it, the second is indifferent and the third dislikes it. Thus the street in the opening shot may represent the world of cinema, the room the mind of Waheed and the pictures painted by him can be taken as a metaphor for his movies (in Urdu, paintings as well as movies were called *'tasveer'*). The three little children represent the entire range of feedback the viewer may offer about the movie at this point: to like it, to be indifferent to it or to dislike it are premature judgment from newcomers. In this sense, those three children become the alter ego of the viewer.

In this way, *Ishara* becomes a coming of age story about the development of the real self – *khudi* – of the viewer. The viewer enters the world of the artist like a child, and soon witnesses the artist falling in love with Aalia (Deeba), a

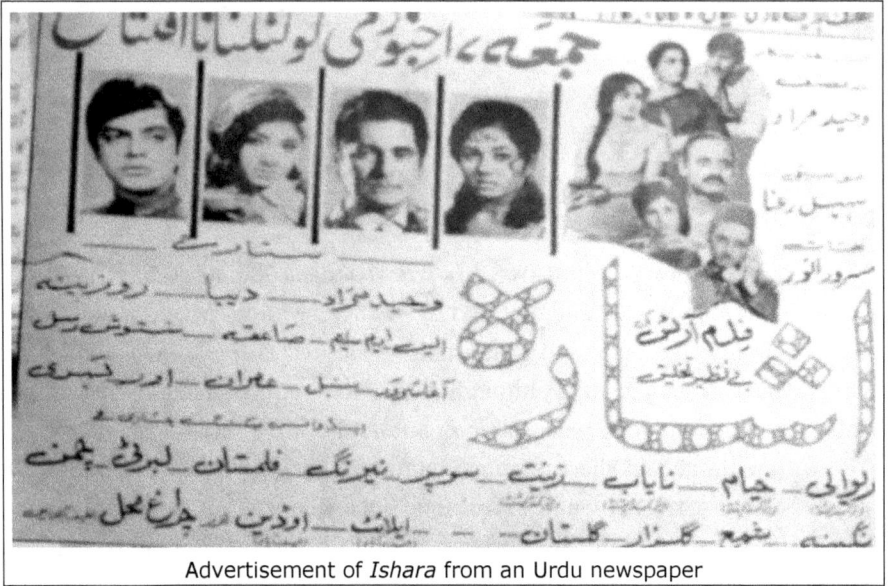

Advertisement of *Ishara* from an Urdu newspaper

college student. At that point, it becomes possible for the viewer to identify himself or herself symbolically with Aalia (which, as we know, was also the name the artist gave in real life to his daughter who was born soon afterwards). Hence 'Aalia' becomes a metaphor for the next generation, of viewers. The artist takes them through a journey into their souls, using those streams of inner thoughts and perceptions that typically pass through one's mind while watching a mainstream movie at the cinema.

Destiny intervenes as the struggling artist gets noticed by Reshma (Rozina), a woman who is young, rich and single. She falls in love with Aamir, but Aamir's heart and soul belong to Aalia. Hence Reshma can represent the artist's contemporaries who were helping him to get recognized in his own times, while the artist remained committed to the posterity. 'I am the Voice of the Poet of Tomorrow,' Iqbal had also said famously. 'Turning away from my contemporaries, I have a word to share with the new generation'.[1]

The posterity, before it could return the artist's love, may have to first resolve some issues of its own. Aalia is under an obligation to marry Ishrat (Talat Husain), the son of her aunt and guardian.

The problem is resolved by Destiny itself, which is not treated here as a cliché but rather as a force that corresponds with the moral strength of a soul.

---

[1] Shafique (2010b)

Rozina as Reshma and Waheed as Aamir – with a portrait of Deeba as Aalia between them – in *Ishara*

This is dramatized in a spectacular sequence of dance and music, which happens in the artist's fantasy, and the film turns from black-and-white to colour at this point. If the mind of the artist had been presented in black and white, his imagination is being depicted in colour: imagination is always so much more colourful.

In that fantasy, a troupe of mysterious dancers leads Aamir into a park. Standing on a lower plane, he observes Aalia at a higher plane. A chorus of eight dancers accompanies each of the two characters, bringing the total number of people on each plane to nine, which is the same as the number of stairs between them.

'My love, do not be sad,' says Aamir as he begins the song (in Urdu), 'You stand on one side, I on the other and the insensitive Time between us.' Ascending the nine steps, he reaches Aalia but the mysterious dancers drag her away from him, and out of the park. The gate closes on him, leaving him trapped inside.

After this grand vision, he comes out of his fantasy and back to his real world where things get sorted out miraculously. Ishrat, who has learnt the truth, unites the lovers dramatically, and they fly off to Islamabad, never to be parted again.

This is how Destiny resolves things, but there might be a catch. The artist has come out of his fantasy but the film did not revert to black and white. It ends in colour. So, is the happy ending an occurrence in the real world, or is it also a part of the artist's fantasy?

The question may be irrelevant if the artist's fantasy is not his alone, but has also become the fantasy of the viewer. The world of imagination is where the viewers are perpetually united with Waheed as an artist, and the meeting is real as long as they both have souls.

Syed Iqbal Hussain Rizvi came up with an unusual idea during a special moment of inspiration. He took it to Waheed, who liked it immediately. This became his next venture, *Naseeb Apna Apna,* released on April 3, 1969. It was directed by Syed Qamar Zaidi. Lyrics were written by Masroor and the music was composed by the duo Lal Muhammad-Iqbal.

In a way, it was a reversal of *Heera Aur Pather,* which Rizvi had written for Waheed five years earlier. Just like Hameed of the previous movie, Javid (Waheed Murad) of *Naseeb Apna Apna* also stays away from his family of humble origins while completing his education. His mother (Tamanna) and older sister, Safiya (Zamarrud), live in Karachi and work hard for financing his education while he studies in Murree. Just like Hameed, Javid also gets the opportunity of reversing his fortune by marrying a woman of wealthy background – Ayesha (Shabnam).

Yet unlike Hameed, he does not hide his humble origins. When Ayesha's wealthy uncle (S. M. Saleem) gives his permission for the marriage on the condition that Javid should live with his in-laws after marriage, Javid refuses for the sake of his mother and sister.

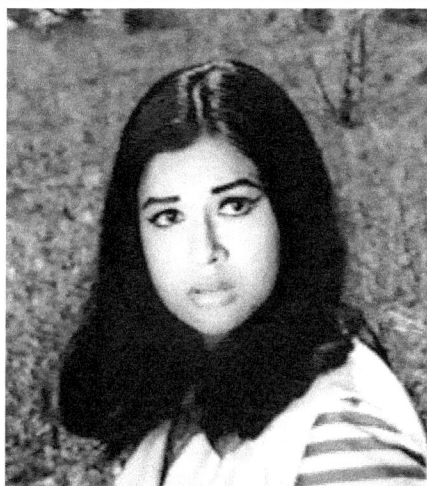

Scenes from *Naseeb Apna Apna.* Clockwise from top left: (a) Shabnam as Ayesha; (b) Waheed as Javid in the disguise of a horse driver; (c) Shabnam and Waheed with S. M. Saleem as Javid's father; (d) Waheed after receiving a heavy slap from Tamanna as mother. Before the take, Waheed had insisted that the slap should be real for maximum impact on the screen.

He has yet to pass a greater test when he discovers that his sister has been working as a dancing girl in the red light district in order to finance his education. (During the shooting of a subsequent scene where Javid accuses his mother and she slaps him, Waheed insisted that Tamanna should slap him for real so that it could come out as more convincing on the screen – and it did!).

If *Heera Aur Pather* was a story of Genesis, here is crucifixion and redemption.

The person responsible for the fall of this family was none other than the father of Javid and Safiya, who married their mother but later abandoned her and the children – evidently a touch of *The Mayor of Casterbridge* by Thomas Hardy, but this 'original sin' of the father is also similar to that of Hameed in *Heera Aur Pather*, who also deserted his blood-relatives. In the climax, Javid confronts his father while cradling the dead body of Safiya in his arms, rather in the manner of Pietà.[1]

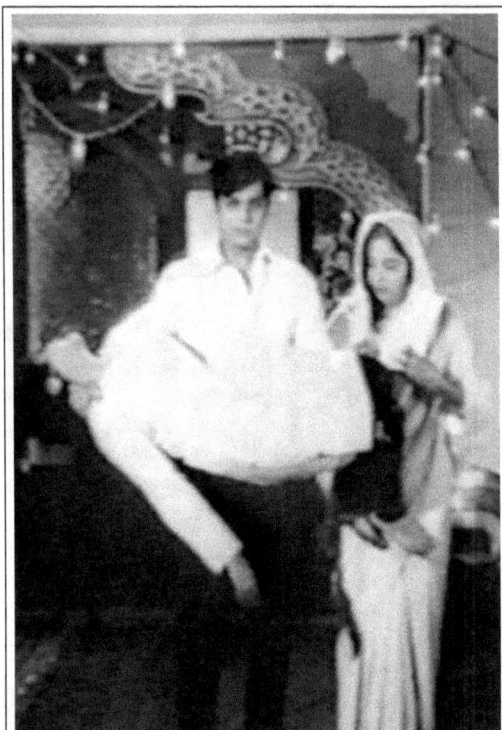

Waheed as Javid and Tamanna as mother with Zamarrud as dead Safiya

British novelist Thomas Hardy, whose character Michael Henchard from *The Mayor of Casterbridge* inspired the character of Javid's father in *Naseeb Apna Apna*.

---

[1] Pietà is the depiction of the Virgin Mary cradling the dead body of Jesus, a common subject in Christian art.

The first general election was held in Pakistan in December 1970, amid great expectations. 'Sohni Dharti', a national song written by Masroor on this occasion, captured the fancy of the nation in melody composed by Sohail and sung by the Bengali singer Shahnaz Begum. 'Jeevay Pakistan' by the poet Jamiluddin Aali, and also composed by Sohail and sung by Shahnaz acquired the same popularity a little after the election. Together, the two songs became a new identity for the nation – significantly in a Bengali voice.

Meanwhile, Awami League led by Sheikh Mujibur Rehman had swept the polls with its Six Points agenda. The support had come exclusively from East Pakistan. The League could not win any seat from the provinces of the West Pakistan, although it had also contested the elections there.

The Pakistan People's Party, led by Zulfikar Ali Bhutto, did not send any candidates from East Pakistan. It was a new party, and unlike the League, it had been founded by an individual. It could not cover most of the country. It suffered a defeat. As compared to 160 seats of the League, it could get only 81 – all from Sindh and Punjab, except one seat from the NWFP (the present-day KPK). It secured none from Balochistan.

A newspaper from West Pakistan after the election of 1970: Bhutto presented as a winner although he had lost.

After losing the election, Bhutto opposed the transfer of power. Protests broke out in East Pakistan and the army stepped in on the night of March 25. Mujib was arrested and transported to West Pakistan where he was kept in custody until the beginning of the next year, while East Pakistan was plunged into a civil war.

This was the backdrop against which the next venture of Film Arts, *Mastana Mahi,* was released on September 24, 1971. The first twenty minutes present a subplot about a village thug preventing a married woman from joining her husband in the other village. One may not find a more apt analogy for the hurdles in the way of the transfer of power to Sheikh Mujib. Political allusions abound throughout this subplot. The skin of a Bengal Tiger is displayed on the wall of the drawing room of the village thug although tiger is not found in Punjab. Someone even remarks about the villain that in his temperament, he resembles some 'foreign country' (apparently India, the self-proclaimed arbiter, who was soon going to launch a military attack). The practical solution presented by the hero to the elders of the village is, 'Why don't you people resolve your matters through consultation with each other?'

'Many people suggested to me that I should work in Punjabi movies,' Waheed recalled the making of *Mastana Mahi* many years later. 'I thought that if that's the case, why shouldn't I produce my first Punjabi film myself so that it will turn out to be a movie according to my liking.'[1]

The complete script – story, dialogue and lyrics – was written by Hazin Qadri, one of the most popular writers of Punjabi. Music was scored by Nazir Ali and the movie was directed by Iftikhar Khan. Since both of them were among the busiest persons in Lahore, Waheed brought them to Karachi and put them up in a hotel to have their exclusive attention. One of the outcomes was the song 'Sayyoni mera mahi', which became phenomenally popular. 'There

---

[1] Statement in the TV show *Silver Jubilee* (Urdu) in 1983. See 'Electronic resources' in the References.

Aliya and Waheed Murad as modern day Heer and Ranjha in *Mastana Mahi*

is a long story behind this song,' the composer Nazir Ali said later. 'When [Hazin] Qadri Sahib gave me the lines … I thought that they were too long; how will they be set to a tune! But then I focused myself on my spiritual mentor Lal Shahbaz Qalandar and imagined that my mentor had come to my house to change my destiny.'[1]

Concerning the correlation between the movie and the social and political circumstance of the time, it is also worth noting that the other hero, Shakil Ahmad (also played by Waheed), is the 'mastana mahi' – the besotted lover – of the title. He comes to the village as a doctor for alleviating the suffering of the poor. His cousin Jamila (Naghma) comes after him but mistakes Raju for him. Raju has always been dreaming about marrying some fashionable woman from the city and he now thinks that his dream has come true. The misunderstanding is resolved quickly but in the meanwhile, Jamila has realized that she would be much happier with Raju than with Shakil. The latter has never been interested in her because he has fancied the simplicity of the village life, and he now finds his match in Raju's cousin Reshma (Aaliya).

These arrangements are unacceptable to the families of Shakil and Jamila. Shakil resolves the mater after discovering that Raju is his step-brother born of the second wife of his late father. Shakil's mother disowned Raju and her mother, and deprived them of their share of the inheritance after the death of

---

[1] The interview of Nazir Ali in PTV show *Mithrey Geet* (Punjabi). See 'Electronic resources' in the References.

Waheed in the double roles of Shakeel and Raju in *Mastana Mahi*

her husband. In a dramatic climax, Shakil prevails upon her mother to acknowledge Raju as the legitimate heir of his father and as a suitable match for Jamila, while he himself returns to Reshma in the village.

This dramatic climax is starkly reminiscent of 'muakhat' – the formation of brotherly bonding on which the foundation of the Muslim society was laid down by the Holy Prophet (peace be upon him). The Prophet had paired each homeless immigrant with one of the residents as brothers, and they treated each other as such. In one instance, the better-off brother is reported to have gone to the extent of offering half of his wealth to his immigrant brother and was also ready to divorce one of his two wives, so that she may marry the newcomer.

This is similar to what happens at the climax of *Mastana Mahi* in a modern setup. Shakil has the choice of marrying either Reshma or Jamila. He chooses Reshma but also ensures that Raju should be recognized as his brother and get married to Jamila. The passionate plea of Shakil on behalf of Raju is something every well-to-do citizen needs to say on behalf of the less privileged fellow-citizens: Look carefully. There is no difference between me and him, except that he could not go to school.

The parallel with the famous story about 'muakhat' is quite obvious. Here also, a wealthy brother shares his wealth with a poor brother and ensures that the poor brother gets marries to one of the two women who are available to the rich brother.

If the long-dead father of Shakil and Raju is replaced with the Quaid-i-Azam – the Father of the Nation – *Mastana Mahi* becomes a parable about Pakistan. All Pakistanis are children of the same father but some have not been recognized as such and are being deprived of their rightful share in the legacy. The most famous song from the movie, 'Sayyoni mera mahi', may then be interpreted as a journey into the deeper recesses of the collective existence.[1]

On December 16, 1971, the Pakistan army surrendered before its Indian counterpart in Dacca [Dhaka]. East Pakistan had already declared independence as Bangladesh on March 26.

Four days after the surrender, Zulfikar Ali Bhutto took control of the remainder of Pakistan as president and chief martial law administrator. He pledged to build 'a new Pakistan' but also 'a Pakistan envisaged by the Quaid-i-Azam'. Could the two be the same?

One possible answer to this question, if one desires, can be sought in *Jaal*, the next venture of Film Arts. It was released on August 31, 1973, soon after the 'new Pakistan' adopted its constitution. The protagonist of *Jaal* is Jahangir (Waheed Murad), a poor taxi driver, who educates his sister Bano (Shaista Qaisar) and gets her married into a well-to-do family. The seemingly noble father-in-law, Seth Harun (S. M. Saleem), accepts the match because – just like the new rulers of the country – he claims that he does not believe in class distinction. It turns out that he is also the ultimate patron of organized crime in the society.

Can our deepest aspirations lead us nowhere except in to the trap – 'jaal' – of respectable thugs? The question is raised by Jahangir with some eloquence at the climax, and the answer offered in the movie is symbolic. The arch criminal has been exposed in a court of law but while the judge is busy writing the judgement, the criminal looks at the picture of the Quaid-i-Azam hanging above the judge, and after a brief eye contact with the picture, he kills himself.

---

[1] Khurram Ali Shafique (2008a)

Should this final triumph be credited to the characters or to the vision of the Quaid – or to both?

Some of the team members from the previous production, *Mastana Mahi,* were retained in *Jaal.* They included Iftikhar Khan as director, Hazin Qadri as the writer of story and dialogue, and Nazir Ali as music director. Lyrics were written by Masroor Anwar and Khwaja Pervez. It was the first venture of Film Arts to be shot entirely in colour. It ran well past a silver jubilee, and was regarded as commercially successful although not as much as had been expected.

Scenes from *Jaal.* Clockwise from top left: (a) Seth Harun (S. M. Saleem); the picture of the Quaid hanging over the judge; (c) Jahangir (Waheed); and (d) Bano (Shaista Qaisar).

The second general election was held in Pakistan in March 1977. Suspicion of rigging by Pakistan People's Party led to widespread protests. The country came on the verge of a second civil war in less than six years. On July 5, General Zia-ul-Haque took control.

Waheed launched his next production, *Hero,* in 1981 – almost seven years after his previous venture. In a press statement about the film, he promised that it would present 'a new Waheed Murad'.[1] The production got delayed due to his subsequent illness and the car accident. It was still unfinished when he passed away in 1983. For a while it was presumed that the movie would not be completed. The soundtrack was released and one of its songs had already become a sensational hit: 'Mil gaye tume to ik yahi gham hai / pyar ziadah hai, zindagi kam hai' ('The only regret after finding you is that love is limitless, and life is short.'). Following enormous pressure from the fan clubs, the film was eventually completed – by using a body double, shooting him only from behind and even leaving out the lines of Waheed in one of the scenes, expecting the audience to figure them out from the dialogue of the other characters).

The movie was released on January 11, 1985. A special message from Salma Murad appeared on a slide before the opening credits. The script had been written by Waheed himself. Director was Iqbal Yusuf,

Cover of the publicity booklet of *Hero*

[1] The present author remembers reading a press statement by Waheed Murad to this effect in the Urdu weekly *Akhbar-i-Jahan* some time before his death.

The premiere of *Hero*. Nayyar Sultana and Salma Murad are visible on the left, Adil in front; and Shirin and Aalia Murad on the right.

the son of S. M. Yusuf who had first introduced Waheed as an actor. Lyrics were from Khwaja Pervez and Masroor Anwar. Music was composed by Kamal Ahmad. The film ran past the silver jubilee and was considered a moderate success.

It presented the story of a thief, Jani (Waheed Murad), who is so perfect in his craft that he leaves no trace behind. This becomes a giveaway, since he is suspected whenever the police fail to find a clue – 'Only Jani can do it with such perfection,' they believe. His boss R. Bukhari (Munawar Saeed) attempts to resolve the problem by setting up a fake film company and introducing an illiterate look alike, Fattoo (also played by Waheed) as a screen hero. The police mistake the look-alike for the thief and keep an eye on him while the thief goes about his business unsuspected.

Hence the question arises of whether the real Waheed Murad was the one whom everybody saw as a screen hero, or the one who remained undiscovered behind the scenes. Whenever Waheed started producing a new movie, Salma would hear him say, 'I have a message to deliver.'[1] The nine messages which he delivered in about twenty years were, however, just a part of his creative output. Two other avenues of his creative activity were writing and acting, respectively the topics of the next two chapters.

---

[1] Reported to the author by Mrs. Salma Murad

94

Chapter 3
The Writer

Out of the nine movies discussed in the previous chapter, Waheed took credit for writing three: *Armaan, Ishara* and *Hero*. Having studied them as movies, we may now treat them as scripts and look at the contribution of Waheed to the literature of his people.

Unfortunately, the academic wisdom of our time informs us about two fundamental categories of literature only. There is the high literature ('adab-i-aalia'), which caters to the educated elite. Then there is popular literature ('awami adab'), which is admittedly aimed at a lower order of interests. The scripts of Waheed cannot be placed in either of these categories because the literary tradition of his society had a third category, uniform literature ('yakrang adab'), where these scripts properly belonged.

A detailed discussion will be offered in the last chapter but here it may be stated briefly that uniform culture was meant to include those works of art and literature which aimed at entertaining the high and the low alike.[1] Although it was banished from Europe at the beginning of the twentieth century, Iqbal considered it indispensable as one of the three components in the structure of his society, the other two being faith and political theory.

The South Asian society in the days of Waheed seemed to demand that a filmmaker should borrow from other contemporary productions – although intelligently. This was not unlike some of the previous phases of European society in which Chaucer borrowed his tales from French authors, and

---

[1] For a detailed discussion of this concept, see Khurram Ali Shafique (2014)

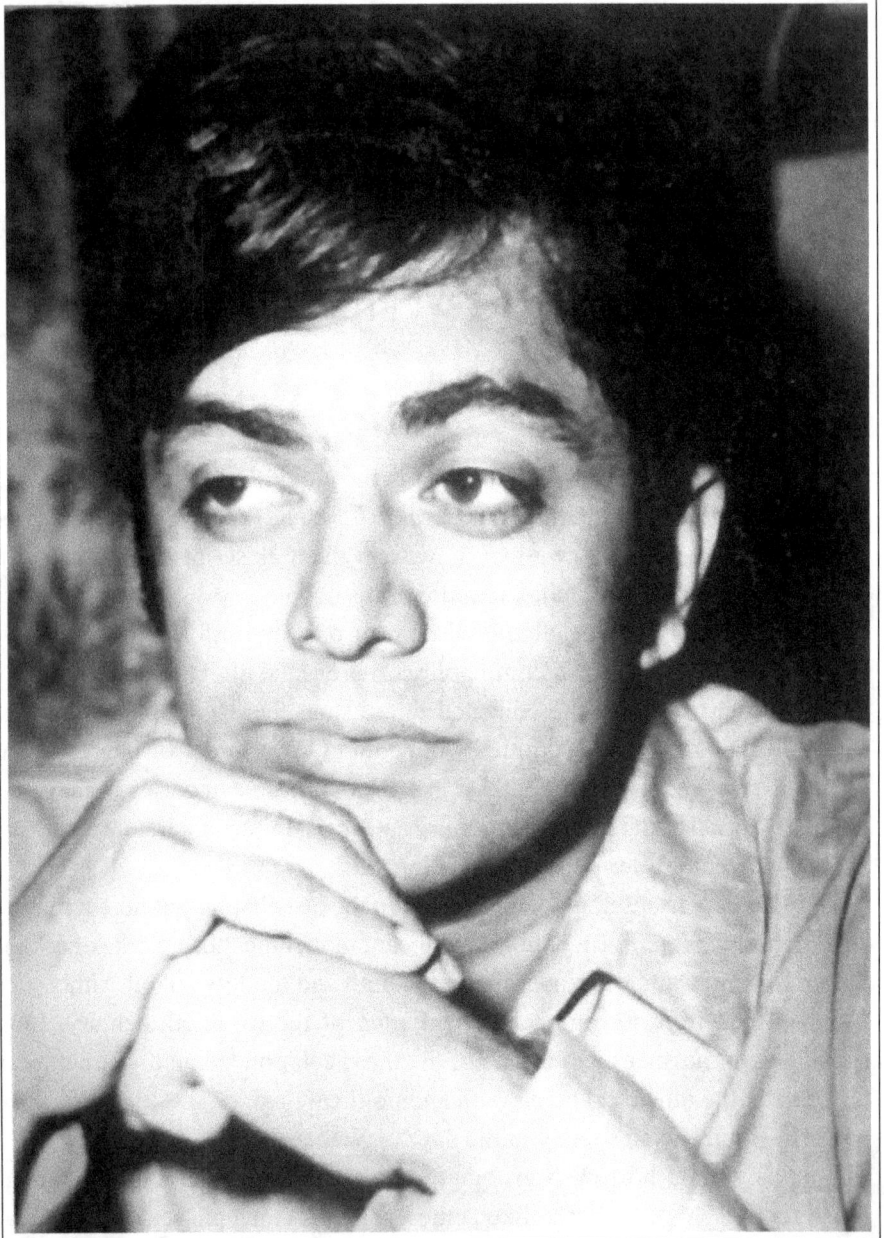

Shakespeare used previously existing material for developing all his plays with the possible exception of the *Tempest.*

As late as 1825, the German poet and thinker Johanne Wolfgang von Goethe prescribed to this practice. 'What is there is mine ... and whether I got it from a book or from life, is of no consequence,' he said. 'The only point is, whether I have made a right use of it.' According to him:

> Walter Scott used a scene from my 'Egmont,' and he had a right to do so; and because he did it well, he deserves praise ... Lord Byron's transformed Devil is a continuation of [my] Mephistopheles, and quite right too. If, from the whim of originality, he had departed from the model, he would certainly have fared worse. Thus, my Mephistopheles sings a song from Shakespeare, and why should he not? Why should I give myself the trouble of inventing one of my own, when this said just what was wanted.[1]

This was because Goethe lived in a society where it could still be said that 'the world remains always the same; situations are repeated; one people lives, loves, and feels like another; why should not one poet write like another? The situations of life are alike; why, then, should those of poems be unlike?'[2]

It is said that the West later moved on to another phase.[3] Such transformation was yet to occur in the society

Johanne Wolfgang von Goethe was presented by Iqbal as a guide for understanding the relationship between culture and society in the modern East in *The Message of the East* (1923).

---

[1] John Oxenford (1883), pp.108-109
[2] John Oxenford (1883), p.107
[3] According to Ian Watts (1957), pp.9-34, this was because belief in 'universals' was displaced with the rise of a mercantile society and various revolutions.

of Waheed. Rather like Goethe, Waheed could still say, *'basically marriage remains the same in past, present or future...'*[1] Listeners in the bazaars in the previous century had demanded of their storytellers to recycle elements from older tales, and the audience of Waheed was no different. Clever screenwriters managed to manipulate the clichés to their own ends – rather like Goethe would have wanted them to. We have already seen some examples in the previous chapter and more will follow here.

Another indicator of the uniqueness of the South Asian mainstream cinema of that period is that it often employed poets of literary acclaim – unlike cinema in the West. In Europe and Hollywood, one could not find outstanding literary names in the credits of mainstream commercial movies. In South Asia, even outside 'art movies' and experimental cinema like that of Satyajit Ray and *The Day Shall Dawn* of the Faiz-Kardar team, contributions from poets of critical acclaim were used in the mainstream movies produced for general consumption. Hafeez Jallundhri, Jigar Muradabadi, Faiz Ahmad Faiz, Shakil Badayuni, Asrar-ul-Haque Majaz, Qateel Shifai, Sahir Ludhianvi, Majrooh Sultanpuri, Ahmad Faraz, Suroor Barabankavi and Javid Akhtar are just some of the names to be cited. Masters from the times before the birth of cinema were also appropriated, such as Mir Taqi Mir, Mirza Ghalib, Bahadur Shah Zafar and others.

Principles for studying the mainstream South Asian cinema of the twentieth century on its own terms are yet to be developed. Until just a dozen years ago, 'the lack of attention paid to Indian popular cinema' was said to be deplorable.[2] Academics seem to be paying more attention to this area now but still nobody has shown how to study South Asian cinema of the twentieth century on its own terms.

Therefore, it is not possible at present to treat the literary contribution of Waheed to an 'analysis of the author's skill in handling the appropriate formal conventions' of a literary model.[3] For now, let's just walk through his writings like an unbiased tourist filled with genuine curiosity.

---

[1] See complete quotation in Chapter 1.
[2] Jyotika Virdi (2003), p.ix
[3] Ian Watt (1957), p.12

In *Armaan*, a student of literature may discern traces of the ancient story of Joseph; the Italian folktale of Cinderella popularized by the French writer Charles Perrault; the Arabic folktale of Laila and Majnu popularized by the Persian poet Nezami Ganjavi; *The Taming of the Shrew* by Shakespeare; *She Stoops to Conquer* by Oliver Goldsmith; *Jane Eyre* by Charlotte Brontë; *Wuthering Heights* by Emily Brontë; *Miratul Uroos* by Deputy Nazeer Ahmad and its upgrade, the movie *Daaman,* by the screenwriter Hasrat Lucknavi. There may also be found points of comparison with Captain Hameed, Qasim and Col. Faridi, the famous characters from the novels of Ibn-e-Safi. One may also add to this list an apparently unintentional resemblance with the Indian film *Majboor* (1964), which was more faithfully adapted by the director Hassan Tariq as *Sawal* (1966) around the same time.

To notice how these diverse influences from the classical and modern East and West come together to create a dramatic symmetry in *Armaan* could be a good start for understanding the structure of a Waheed Murad movie.

We may notice, for instance, that the two halves of the movie mirror each other in many ways. In the first half, Nasir pulls a prank on Najma by swapping his identity with his friend Shahid (something like *She Stoops to Conquer* by Oliver Goldsmith).[1] In the second half, Najma swaps her innocence with the guilt of Seema, although with less comic effect.

Through such devices, elements in the plot of *Armaan* are held together so tightly that the movie does not fail to grip its viewers even half a century later. Unlike most of its contemporaries, it refuses to become 'dated'.

Najma stands out as a heroine who remains in control of the things happening around her almost throughout. While she is being ridiculed and

---

[1] In *She Stoops to Conquer* (1773), Charles Marlow is sent by his rich Londoner father to court Kate Hardcastle, the daughter of a family friend who lives in the countryside. Marlow feels nervous in the company of upper-class women but not so with the working-class women, and therefore Kate meets him in the disguise of a working-class woman. A subplot involves courtship between Marlow's friend George Hastings (who is accompanying him just like Shahid accompanies Nasir in *Armaan*), and Kate's cousin, Constance Neville. See Oliver Goldsmith (1917).

Najma, the heroine of *Armaan* and her literary ancestors. From top to bottom and from left to right: (a) Najma (played by Zeba); (b) Persian poet Nezami Ganjavi; (c) English playwright William Shakespeare; (d) French writer Charles Perrault; (e) English playwright Oliver Goldsmith; (f) English novelist Charlotte Brontë; (g) English novelist Emily Brontë; (h) Urdu novelist Deputy Nazeer Ahmad; and (i) Urdu screenwriter Hasrat Lucknavi, whose *Daaman* seems to be an important link in the genesis of the character on the indigenous side from Deputy Nazeer Ahmad' *Miratul Uroos* to Waheed Murad's *Armaan*.

rejected by her loved ones, the audience remains aware that this is by choice and she can change the situation whenever she likes. In this sense at least, she can be considered as a personification of Destiny.[1]

If this is an achievement, Waheed may have been happy to share the laurels with many authors who preceded him. His creation, Najma, may have been the final stage in the evolution of some of the best-loved heroines from around the world:

- Najma is Cinderella, because she is an orphaned girl living with an unkind aunt and selfish cousins, and she finds her prince in Nasir.[2]
- She is also one of the 'later lives' of Jane Eyre.[3] In spite of being in love with Rochester, Brontë's heroine turns away because she learns that Rochester is already married.[4] Najma also turns away from Nasir but in this case, the other woman marries the hero afterwards. Hence it is Najma who knows the dark secret associated with the hero's marriage while the hero himself is unaware – unlike Jane, who knew less than Rochester. Najma's return to Nasir at the climax of the movie, immortalized by the song 'Akele na jana', parallels the return of Jane to Rochester at the end of that book – 'too awful and inexplicable to be communicated or discussed'[5]
- Najma also mirrors certain aspects of Catherine Earnshaw, the enigmatic heroine of *Wuthering Heights* by Emily Brontë. Her mysterious appearances before Nasir after being presumed dead are so reminiscent of Catherine haunting Heathcliff from her the other world: 'In every cloud, in every tree—filling the air at night, and caught by glimpses in every object by day—I am surrounded with her image!'

---

[1] In 'Jane Eyre in Later Lives: Intertextual Strategies in Women's Self-Definition' – anthologized in Elsie B. Michie (Ed.; 2006), pp.177-194 – Patsy Stoneman argues with examples from women's writings from the 20th Century that 'Jane's significant legacy lies not in her attainment of the object of her desire—experience or love—but in her control of the process of writing.' This is because the novel is narrated by Jane in the first person, but how to translate this into a movie? Perhaps *Armaan* is the answer.
[2] The earliest written version appears in *Pentamerone* (1634), a Neapolitan classic by Giambattista Basile. The better-known version – with pumpkin, fairy godmother and glass slipper – comes from the French author Charles Perrault (1697). See Giambattista Basile (2007) and Charles Perrault (2009).
[3] This is a reference to 'Jane Eyre in Later Lives: Intertextual Strategies in Women's Self-Definition' by Patsy Stoneman, anthologized in Elsie B. Michie (Ed.; 2006), pp.177-194.
[4] Charlotte Brontë (1971/2001), pp. 246-274
[5] Charlotte Brontë (1971/2001), p.381

Mirroring of situations is one of the devices through which elements in the plot of *Armaan* are held together. After his first encounter with Najma, Nasir looks her up in the kitchen to have a conversation – as seen in the top picture. When he arrives disguised as his father, he again meets her in the kitchen, and repeats the same conversation, much to her bafflement.

- Najma is obviously comparable with the legendary Laila, immortalized by the Persian poet Nezami Ganjavi. Nasir himself compares his love for Najma with the love of Majnu for Laila.[1]
- Najma is also a successor of Asghari, the famous character introduced by the Urdu writer Deputy Nazeer Ahmed in the nineteenth century.

Seema, the cousin who is the source of Najma's troubles, is also a more sophisticated version of the vamps from some of the stories mentioned here –

[1] Unintentionally perhaps, 'Akele na jana' sung by Najma at the climax approximates the gist of the letter written by Laila to Qays in Nezami's poem. The most famous line in that letter is, '[God] is the companion of those who have no other friend' [Nezami Ganjavi (1966), p.161]. This has also turned up in the song: 'Hai jin ka nahin koi un ka Khuda hai.'

stepsisters of Cinderella; Bertha, the madwoman in *Jane Eyre;* and Akbari in *Miratul Uroos.* Unlike the stepsisters of Cinderella, Seema is capable of extending sympathy but just like them, she ends up as Najma's rival. Just as Bertha puts her house on fire, Seema also endangers hers. Like Bertha, she also commits suicide during the catastrophe – although by taking poison rather than by jumping off the roof.[1]

Seema is attractive – unlike Bertha, who was a 'clothed hyena'.[2] Still, it could be said about her what was said about Bertha: 'she is so cunning: it is not in mortal discretion to fathom her craft.'[3] Her 'madness' is more subtle than Bertha's, though, and resembles what is now called borderline personality disorder (BPD).

In Urdu literature, Deputy Nazeer Ahmad introduced 'the mirrors for women' genre with *Mirat-ul Uroos* (*Bride's Mirror*) in 1869.[4] The objective was 'to instruct young girls in the conduct of a virtuous family life.'[5] Typically, this was achieved through comparison between two a 'good woman' and a 'bad woman'. In the prologue and the epilogue of *Daaman,* Waheed's second movie as an actor, the screenwriter Hasrat Lucknavi, appeared on screen with a guest artist and explained this concept for the benefit of the audience. The heroine in that movie was named Najma (played by Sabiha Khanum), and Waheed's character was the husband of the evil woman, not unlike Nasir in the second half of *Armaan.*

Together, *Daaman* and *Armaan* modified the older point of view which had identified virtue with education, and evil with illiteracy.

Nasir, like the character of Waheed in *Daaman,* is introduced to the viewers as a handsome young man who enjoys floor dancing but his matrimonial ideals are quite different from the other one. The character displays many ingredients form Waheed's own personality and worldview – evenings out in Karachi, long drives to Murree, practical jokes, and a fairly conventional

---

1 Charlotte Brontë (1971/2001), pp.364-365: '...she was on the roof; where she was standing, waving her arms, above the battlements, and shouting out till they could hear her a mile off; I saw her and heard her with my own eyes. She was a big woman, and had long black hair: we could see it streaming against the flames as she stood. I witnessed, and several more witnessed Mr. Rochester ascend through the skylight on to the roof: we heard him call "Bertha!" We saw him approach her; and then, ma'am, she yelled, and gave a spring, and the next minute she lay smashed on the pavement.'
2 Charlotte Brontë (1971/2001), p.250
3 Charlotte Brontë (1971/2001), p.250
4 Deputy Nazeer Ahmad (n.d.).
5 Meenakshi Mukherjee (2002/2005), p.131

Zeba and Tarranum as Najma and Seema in *Armaan*

view about the institution of marriage. Outside the biography of Waheed, the conscious or unconscious sources of the character could have been:

- Majnu, the hero of Nezami's poem, was omnipresent in the culture of the region, and as mentioned earlier, Nasir compares himself with that character.
- Since 1952, the novelist Ibn-e-Safi had emerged as the most popular writer in Urdu since Iqbal. Two of his main characters, Col. Faridi and Capt. Hameed, dominated the imagination of the society at that time. Nasir reflects the traits of both: he is playful like Capt. Hameed and principle-centered like Col. Faridi. His very entry on the screen – with the song 'Kokokorina' – is reminiscent of Capt. Hameed's outings in High Circle Night Club, where Hameed dates women without getting seriously involved and dances on the floor but refrains from taking alcohol. The way Nasir pulls the strings of his stooge Shahid by giving him the hope of finding a romantic liaison is also quite similar to how Capt. Hameed handles Qasim.[1]

---

[1] For analyses of these characters, see Khurram Ali Shafique (Urdu; 2011b), pp.105-118, 129-139, 164-172. For anecdotes about Qasim, see Khurram Ali Shafique (Urdu; 2011a), pp.143-149 and 176-201.

- Nasir's disguise as his own father is reminiscent of the subplot in *The Taming of the Shrew* involving Lucentio and Bianca, where Lucentio's father Vincentio is impersonated but the farce is exposed with the arrival of the real Vincentio.[1]

The purpose of *Armaan*, according to Sohail Rana, was to portray the gradual self-discovery of Nasir:

The point in *Armaan* is that it is the story of a young boy who is modern, and likes to go out to clubs. And what used to happen in those clubs was rock 'n' roll, foxtrot, twist. If he sings a song there, [it should have] a western

Nasir (Waheed) disguised as his father

touch, western beat, western instruments. That is what we did to 'Kokokorina'. But we kept its background a bit oriental. 'Kokokorina' was meant to depict the boy's character as we find him at the beginning of the story. As he matures through falling in love with a girl, he undergoes a reformation. Now he is not a visitor of the clubs; he does not take his beloved to the club, nor does he want such a girl as his beloved. So, now he expresses his emotion through 'Akele na jana', which is based on raga Aiman. This song embodies our own art, our own values, our own metaphors. Later, when that same boy goes back to the club, he is singing a different song. Things at the club appear to him as false shadows ('Saye ki talab karney walo') and he expresses himself in raga Bhopali: 'Jab pyar main do dil miltay hain'. Now, this song is a long way from Kokokorina. You see, I have made the same character sing three different types of songs

---

[1] William Shakespeare (1981/2003), Act. IV, Sc. 2, 4, 6; and Act. V, Sc.1. This had also been echoed in *She Stoops to Conquer* where the arrival of the protagonist's father puts an end to 'the mistakes of a night'.

Waheed Murad as Nasir – haunted by the 'ghost' of Najma – in *Armaan*

at three different phases in his life [and] I have given you justification for each one.'[1]

This was not a lens to be used by the literary critics of the times. In one of the earliest references to *Armaan,* which appeared in 'Film Notes' in *Dawn* soon after the release of the movie, it was said that 'there is nothing here by way of story.' Elements that were likely to be appreciated by the sophisticated audience were pointed out very insightfully, and the genre correctly identified as melodrama. Surprisingly though, the script was still blamed for following conventions that had long been accepted as legitimate in that genre even in Europe.

FILM NOTES

by Dawn Film Critic[2]

Filmarts' latest production, ARMAAN (Naz) is an entertaining melodrama which has been intelligently directed and well acted. A good musical score is the feature of the film. Its cast consists of Zeba,

---

[1] Khurram Ali Shafique (1996 b)
[2] I am thankful to my friend Akhtar Wasim Dar for retrieving it for me.

Waheed Murad, Nirala, Bibbo, Tarannum [Tarranum] and Rozina among others. Music is by Sohail Rana.

Written by Waheed Murad himself, there is nothing here by way of story but director Pervez Malik's competent handling of the script gives it a fresh look. The exhilarating proceedings of the first half are also aided by good performances by Zeba, Waheed Murad and Nirala who clown, dance and sing their way to one's heart and the romantic interludes become the film's highlight.

The second half, however, gets crammed with too many 'stock' situations. But the theme song, 'Akele Na Jana' rendered powerfully by Mala, provides the much-needed 'tonic' before the fade out, and the film pulls out of the wood with a melodramatic bravado.

'Melodramatic bravado' may be an understatement for what *Armaan* achieves for melodrama. In order to fade out with the last song, the wind-up has been placed before the climax. Before the last song, Najma is discovered by Shahid and brought home for reconciliation with her aunt and with Nasir's father. This is all the wind up there should be, and the story practically ends here except that Nasir has gone out to jump off a hill because he thinks that Najma is dead. So Najma goes after him and when she announces her presence to him with a larger than life song, the audience has no further information to take in. In three and half minutes the song offer the viewer an experience where nothing is to be understood, and therefore the will triumphs over the mind. The mind is held in abeyance and the viewer becomes nothing except the will. This, incidentally, was the purpose for which the French thinker Jean-Jacques Rousseau invented melodrama in 1762 with his *Pygmalion,* but this purpose may never have been achieved more effectively than in *Armaan.*

The French thinker
Jean-Jacques Rousseau,
the inventor of melodrama

The second movie written by Waheed was *Ishara*. The title literally means clue, signal, gesture, allusion, hint or suggestion. This is important if the script is to be studied as an outcome of Waheed's fascination with James Joyce, since the use of allusions is very prominent in the work of Joyce and has been noted for 'its extent and thoroughness'.[1]

In the previous chapter, *Ishara* has already been discussed as a story about the development of the viewer's ego. In that sense, it is a dramatic relative of the 'formation novel' ('Bildungsroman'), which deals with the formation of an individual personality through interplay between character and environment – and not social or biological determination, nor through mere acquisition of knowledge and technical skills.[2] The personality to be formed in *Ishara* is the viewer herself or himself – symbolically represented by Aalia in the story. The development of this character is aimed at the achievement of complete harmony.

This is obviously different from the worldview presented by James Joyce in his formation novel, *A Portrait of the Artist as A Young Man*. The Joycean worldview is summarized in the famous quote: 'You talk to me of nationality, language, religion. I shall try to fly by those nets.'[3]

The Joycean type of artist is represented in *Ishara* by Bezar (literally meaning 'Fed Up'). An unsuccessful classical singer, he is also Aamir's neighbour and best friend. In his fantasy, he finds himself performing a pop song, rather like Fred Astaire. The lyrics of the song translate as 'There is none like me in this whole big world.' Indeed, everybody in the fantasy is a manifestation of Bezar's ego (played by the same actor) – from musicians in

---

[1] Weldon Thornton (1961/1973), p.4
[2] This definition has been derived from the argument presented by Manfred Engel in 'Variants of the Romantic "Bildungsroman" (with a short note on the "artist novel")', included in Gerald Gillespie, et. al. (Ed.; 2008), pp.263-295. Most famous examples include *The Apprenticeship of Wilhelm Meister* (*Wilhelm Meisters Lehrjahre* in German) by Goethe than *A Portrait of the Artist as a Young Man* by James Joyce, while a precursor has been identified in the medieval Arabic work, *Hayy ibn Yaqdhan* by Ibn-i-Tufail.
[3] James Joyce (1916), p.238

the orchestra to the high-brow audience, and even the women. Still, Bezar is in conflict with some of these manifestations of himself!

By contrast, Aamir's very first song is a song of thanksgiving, attributing a recently achieved success to the Grace of the Almighty, and sharing his happiness with everyone. Dancing in the street, he pulls together the entire range of society from burqa-clad women to girls in tight trousers, and from the roadside worker to men in evening suits – people belonging to three successive generations of children, youth and seniors. First bringing them together in pairs, Aamir then makes them dance in a moving circle while he revolves in the centre, not unlike a whirling dervish of Rumi or a dhammal dancer of Shahbaz Qalandar. Gradually, he slips away but the circle keeps moving.

In spite of his great admiration for the creative genius of Joyce, Waheed turns out to be a different type of artist in his self-revelation. What Carlyle wrote about Goethe in the previous century could also be said about Aamir:

He is neither noble nor plebeian, neither liberal nor servile, nor infidel nor devotee; but the best excellence of all these, joined in pure union; 'a clear and universal Man.' ... To our minds, in these soft, melodious imaginations of his, there is embodied the Wisdom which is proper to this time; the beautiful, the

Top to bottom: (a) the classical singer Bezar (Lehri), representative of the high culture; (b) in his fantasy, Bezar sees himself as a pop singer; (c) the orchestra comprises his own images; and (d) and so does the audience.

The artist of uniform culture: Amir (Waheed) seeks opinion on his painting from three children

religious Wisdom, which may still, with something of its old impressiveness, speak to the whole soul; still, in these hard, unbelieving utilitarian days, reveal to us glimpses of the Unseen but not unreal World, that so the Actual and the Ideal may again meet together, and clear Knowledge be again wedded to Religion, in the life and business of men.[1]

With a 'living and life-giving harmony', which is the gift of such an artist,[2] Waheed guides the viewer on a journey into their own souls, and reveals that there cannot be any evil in those depths. In *Ishara,* there is no villain.

'The conception of the modern world in a single work of art' was said to be an achievement of James Joyce in *Ulysses.*[3] 'A line-by-line reference' to its allusions takes up a volume of approximately 550 pages of small print.[4]

---

[1] Introduction to Johann Wolfgang von Goethe (1882/1901), p.iii-iv
[2] *Ibid.* p.v
[3] Hermann Broch (1936) quoted by Ehrhard Bahr in Hardin (1999).
[4] This is a reference to Weldon Thornton (1961/1973).

A similar guide to *Ishara* will probably take just as many pages. Some of these allusions involve photographs of celebrities. In one of the comic scenes, where Aamir and the warden of Aalia's hostel are engaged in a shouting match, the photograph of a smiling Jinnah hangs on the wall behind them and is shot at such an angle that it seems as if the Quaid is amused by the funny situation, just like

A smiling Quaid watches over an angry warden.

the audience. Pictures of the legendary Indian singers Lata Mangeshkar and Muhammad Rafi, and the Pakistani legend Noor Jahan are used in a similar manner in another comic scene where the issue at hand is music.

Other allusions may be found embedded in the music and embellishment. When the movie transforms from black and white to colour, the note of music heard in the background is reminiscent of the opening note in the title music of *Aan*, the first colour movie of South Asia.

Some of the gestures of Aamir in the movie are strikingly reminiscent of the iconic movements of Waheed himself from his other films (e.g. his running towards Aalia upon meeting her after a long gap is so visibly a reference to the famous last moments of *Armaan*).

There also seems to be a subtle allusion to Hollywood musicals, where the actors usually sang their own songs. Waheed and Deeba do that in *Ishara*, and the ending of the song is reminiscent of the most iconic song of all

Amir (Waheed) singing from a public telephone in *Ishara,* as yet unaware of the constable who has appeared on the right.

Hollywood musicals, 'Singin' in the Rain' from the movie of the same name. In *Singin' in the Rain,* the character of Gene Kelly is singing on a street past midnight when he finds himself being watched by a suspicious police constable. In *Ishara,* Amir uses a public telephone outside the post office for singing his song at late night, and a suspicious police constable appears in the end.

The most striking allusion – standing out as the very foundation of the story – is to the fiction writer Ibn-e-Safi. The very unusual coincidence through which Aalia and Aamir meet for the first time is adapted from the opening chapters of the Ibn-e-Safi novel *Baibakoan Ki Talash.*

Although there is no record of communication between Waheed and Ibn-e-Safi, it is interesting to note that when Ibn-e-Safi decided to adapt one of his novels for the screen, he also picked up the same book – out of more than a hundred which he had written by then. Waheed paid a special visit to the sets of this movie, *Dhamaka,* while it was being shot at the Eastern Films Studios.

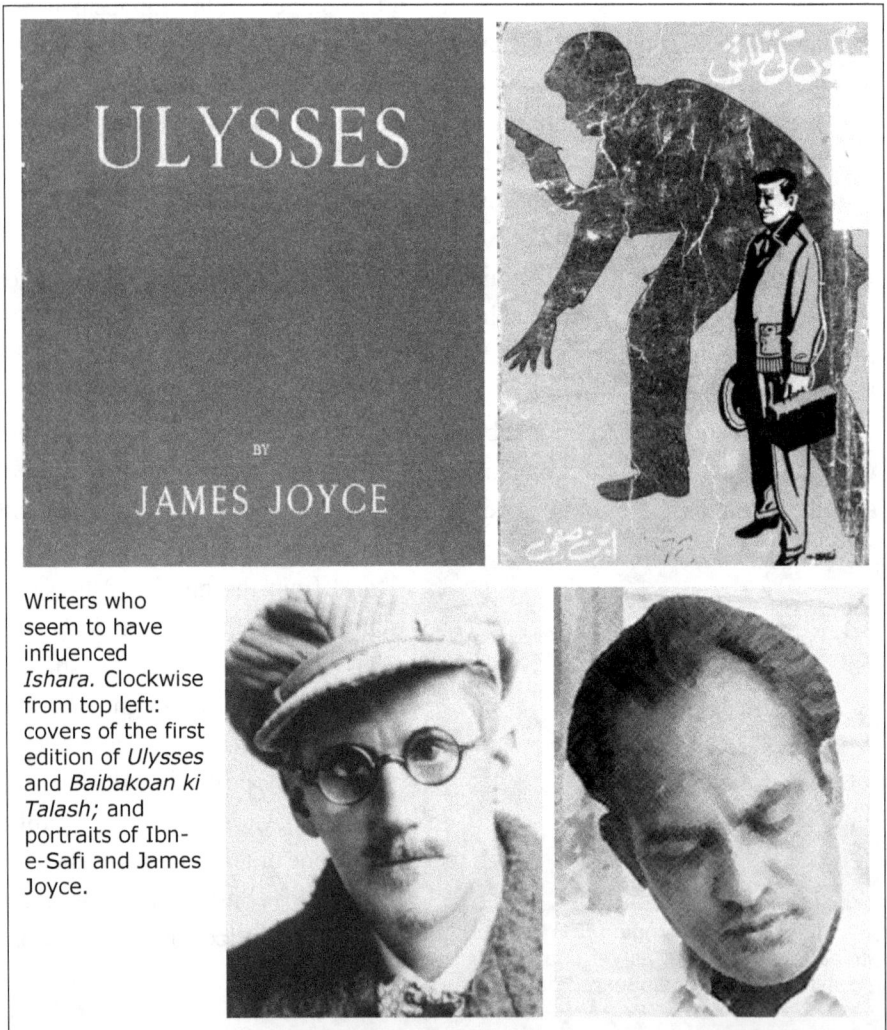

Writers who seem to have influenced *Ishara.* Clockwise from top left: covers of the first edition of *Ulysses* and *Baibakoan ki Talash;* and portraits of Ibn-e-Safi and James Joyce.

If *Ishara* presents the imagined world of the artist from within, *Hero* shows it from the outside. As discussed in the previous chapter, *Hero* is a movie about the making of movies. The world behind the scenes is presented on the screen here.

If *Ishara* was the self-revelation of the viewer, *Hero* is the self-revelation of the filmmaker. In the movie, characters even talk about 'Waheed Murad' as a celebrity.

Taking lead from these, a viewer may like to spot the more subtle allusions to other movies of Waheed, especially the ones produced by him. The long-lost brothers in *Hero* – Fattoo and Jani – are similar to Raju and Shakil from *Mastana Mahi* in some ways. Fattoo's attempt to disguise himself as his own father is reminiscent of the similar gag in *Armaan*. The mother of Fattoo and Jani comes from the village to the city looking for her sons, just like the father in *Heera Aur Pather*. Due to these and many other allusions, *Hero* allows itself to be interpreted as a parable about the career of Waheed as an artist.

As mentioned earlier, the popularity of the Indian movies in Pakistan endangered the very survival

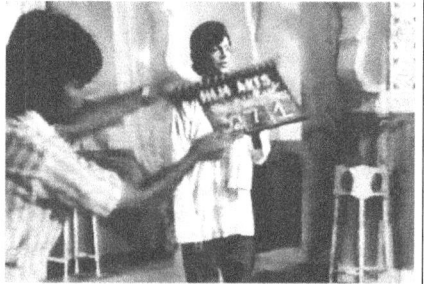

Inside-out: in *Hero*, the world behind the scenes is presented on screen. Top to bottom: (a) Jani and Fattoo discuss the concept of body double; (b) clapper board; (c) director, crew, security and producer.

113

The wannabe star Fattoo (Waheed) tries to prove his talent by mimicking 'Waheed Murad' before the film star Shola (Mumtaz) in *Hero*

of the industry Waheed and his father had helped create. In *Hero,* the very first peek inside a Pakistani film studio discloses a song and dance sequence being imitated from the Indian blockbuster *Sholay* (1976).

There was a time when Waheed used to defend the native industry almost unconditionally. To the common objection that the Pakistani films were not realistic because they were all about courtship and romance, he had replied, 'Of course our films are realistic. What could be more realistic than falling in love and getting married?'[1] The manner in which the film trade deteriorated after the break-up of Pakistan left Waheed feeling very bitter as was also evident from his remarks in the TV show *Silver Jubilee,* mentioned in Chapter 1.

Consequently, in *Hero,* one finds the movie industry to be in a sorry state and infiltrated by people from the underworld.

---

[1] The author remembers reading this in an old issue of *Eastern Films* from the late 1960s or the early 1970s, but unfortunately the files of that magazine could not be accessed now.

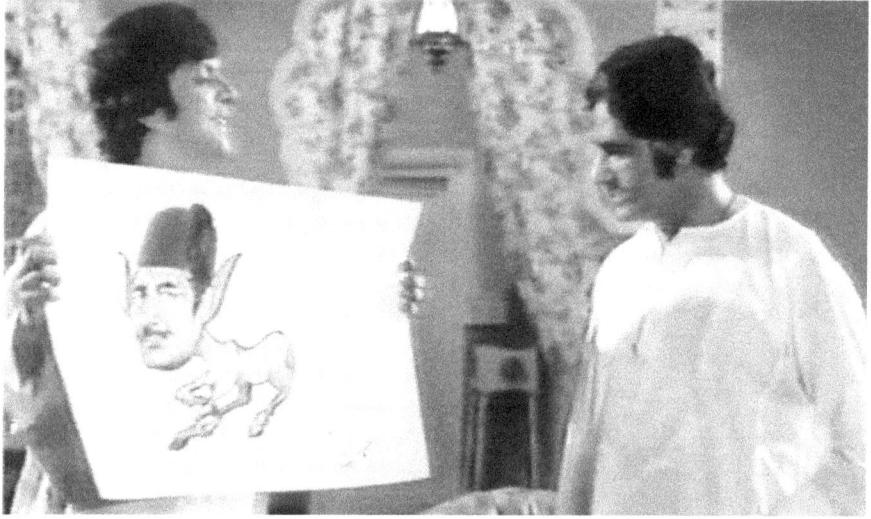

Waheed and Lehri in a lighter moment in *Hero*

This was true. Personalities with criminal records were investing in movies. This was also reflected in the choice of subjects.[1] Maula Jatt, a vigilante hero conceived by the Marxist writer Ahmad Nadeem Qasmi, had become a popular trend in Punjabi movies, glorifying crime and violence. Pervez Malik had already come out with a strong protest against it through his movie *Rishtaa* (1980) – with story, dialogue and songs from Masroor Anwar. The protagonist in *Rishtaa,* played by Nadeem, makes a passionate plea against the rising trend:

> This is our misfortune. We are giving birth to a society where courage has become synonymous with crime, and to be noble is to be seen as a coward. Today, a blood-dripping *gandasa* has become the icon of our culture and civilization, instead of the reed emanating the melodies of love. Please think, what have we made of this beautiful land [*Sohni Dharti*] of Heer and Ranjha?'[2]

It seems that in *Hero,* Waheed was on the same page with his old friends. His last bow was nothing short of a stand against the culture of lawlessness and despair, which had begun to overpower the film trade after poisoning the minds of the intellectuals and the academics for two generations.

---

[1] See Hashim Bin Rashid & Sher Khan (2012).
[2] See Khurram Ali Shafique (2012c)

Director Shabab Keranvi, Salma Murad, film star Deeba and Waheed on the outdoor shooting of *Tumhi Ho Mehboob Mere*

Chapter 4
The Chocolate-Cream Hero

A s mentioned earlier, Waheed made an uncredited cameo appearance in *Saathi* (1959), but his first acting role was in *Aulad* (1962). The movie was directed by S. M. Yusuf, who was also a co-producer.[1] Waheed's last acting role was in *Zalzala* (1987), released posthumously. It was directed and co-produced by Iqbal Yusuf, the son of the person who had introduced Waheed as an actor twenty-five years earlier.

The first three assignments of Waheed as an actor were in supporting roles. In all three, he was presented as an educated young man with sophisticated manners, and seemed to be in danger of being typecast. Shaukat Hashmi, a film director from those days, later recalled, 'I was looking for a hero who would look well educated. Qadeer Ghauri suggested to me to sign Waheed Murad.'

Hashmi's account of casting Waheed for *Doctor* (1965) provides a vivid picture of Waheed's professionalism as an actor. According to Hashmi:

I called Waheed's father Nisar Murad in Karachi. He said that Waheed would be coming to his office soon; it would be better if I speak to him directly. When I called again after two hours, Waheed was in the office and was awaiting my call. I told him that I could pay him only fifteen

---

[1] *Aulad* has always been regarded as his debut. The cameo was all but forgotten until mentioned in recent years by sources such as the website Mazhar.dk . When the present author asked Syed Iqbal Hussain Rizvi, the writer of *Saathi,* he recalled the cameo only vaguely. The copy of the movie available on DVD is so bad that sometimes the faces are not recognizable. Waheed may have been the operator who appears in a factory scene, working on a machine.

thousand rupees and will pay it lump sum before the release [of the movie]. I would require 12 consecutive shifts from him. These would comprise of some days and some nights. Waheed would have to bring four suits and a few bush shirts, trousers, etc., of his own because I did not have the time for getting new clothes made for him.[1] Then I told him that his role was that of a young doctor. Waheed kept listening silently. When I stopped, he said, 'I accept your offer but I also have a few terms of my own.' I inquired about his conditions and he said, 'I shall not come by night coach [cheaper than day-time flights at that time]. Pay me five thousands on my arrival in Lahore and the remaining ten thousand before the release, as you have suggested. I shall stay at some decent hotel during the shoot – whichever you choose from the Faletti's, Ambassador or International.'

I accepted all three terms of his. On the morning of the appointed day, I received him at the airport and lodged him in the Ambassador Hotel. He had a shooting the next day. His work was only on four sets. I had got them all constructed on various floors of Shahnoor Studios. A duet had to be filmed on him and Bahar in the grove of trees behind Shahnoor Studios. I had made arrangements for that too. A closing shot of the film had to be filmed against the backdrop of sunset. I had chosen a location near Shahnoor for that too, and had scheduled it.

When I reached the Ambassador [Hotel] in my car at 7 am the next morning, Waheed was strolling in the lawn outside and was waiting for us ... I completed this movie in 35 shifts, including the ten shifts of Waheed. I had booked him for 12 shifts but his work was completed in 10 due to his cooperation and punctuality, and he returned quietly to Karachi on the eleventh day without making any demands or giving any reminder [about the payment].[2]

---

[1] Clothes were usually tailor made at that time.

[2] Written on the occasion of Waheed's death in 1983, and included in S. A. Najam (n.d.). It seems that his memory didn't serve him well about some details (not included here), e.g. he writes that S. M. Yusuf cast Waheed after watching the rush prints of *Doctor,* while *Daaman* had already been released. The chronology of these movies does not allow this possibility.

His decision to play the character of a donkey cart driver in his first lead role – in his own production *Heera Aur Pather* – may have been motivated partially by a desire to do a different type of role than his earlier movie, but he reprised the sophisticated role in his next venture, *Armaan.* The phenomenal success of that movie landed him with more assignments of a similar nature. His roles in his 125 movies can be divided into five categories – or his five personas, if we may call them so.[1]

His character in his first movie, *Aulad,* was named Amaan (literally meaning 'peace' or 'amnesty'). Brought up by a poor but upright mother who lived by the philosophy of Iqbal, Amaan was presented as a role model to be

Waheed Murad in his debut role in *Aulad*

---

[1] Khurram Ali Shafique (1993b)

emulated by the youth. In other movies of Waheed, this type of educated and well-mannered young man, while struggling for success, is often called upon to make some sacrifice for a higher purpose, such as family or profession. Waheed's own production *Ehsaan* is perhaps the best example.[1] Other instances include *Kaneez, Honhaar, Insaniyat, Dewar Bhabhi, Doraha, Phir Subha Hogi, Maan Baap, Dil Mera Dharkan Teri, Ishara, Ma Beta, Naseeb Apna Apna, Chand Suraj, Neend Hamari Khwab Tumhare, Mulaqat, Nannah Farishta, Dushman, Saheli, Gunman, Dil Ney Phir Yaad Kiya* and *I Love You*.

The five personas of Waheed Murad

Clockwise from top right: (a) the struggling graduate; (b) the wealthy young man; (c) the sinister character; (d) the unschooled mind; and (e) costume.

---

[1] It has already been discussed in Chapters 1 and 2.

In his second movie, *Daaman*, his character, Aslam, also had good education and good manners but unlike Amaan he came from wealthy background. This type of character did not have to struggle for a career but went straight ahead to self-discovery through the pains of a relationship. Best example, of course, is *Armaan*.[1] Other instances include *Bahu Begum, Bhaiya, Jahan Tum Wahan Hum, Salgirah, Tumhi Ho Mehboob Mere, Ladla, Andaleeb, Anjuman, Afsana, Be Wafa, Rim Jhim, Afshan, Khamosh Nigahain, Naag Muni, Bandagi, Zindagi Aik Safar Hai, Tum Salamat Raho, Phool Mere Gulshan Ka, Mastani Mahbooba, Haqeeqat, Anhoni, Shama, Izzat, Soorat Aur Seerat, Dil Ruba, Zubeda, Rastey Ka Pather, Mehboob Mera Mastana, Mohabbat Zindgi Hai, Zaib-un-Nisa, Kharidar, Jio Aur Jeene Do, Shabana, Aap Ka Khadim, Parastish, Aadmi, Waade Ki Zanjeer, Tarana, Nishani, Zamir, Bandhan, Piyari, Kiran Aur Kali, Aahat* and *Maang Meri Bhar Do*.

He picked a movie from this category when asked to name his personal favourite in the TV show *Silver Jubilee*. '*Anjuman*,' he said, 'in my judgement was a fairly perfect movie. Fairly perfect in the sense of its story, character, music, choreography, set, direction – I did not find any flaw in that movie.'[2]

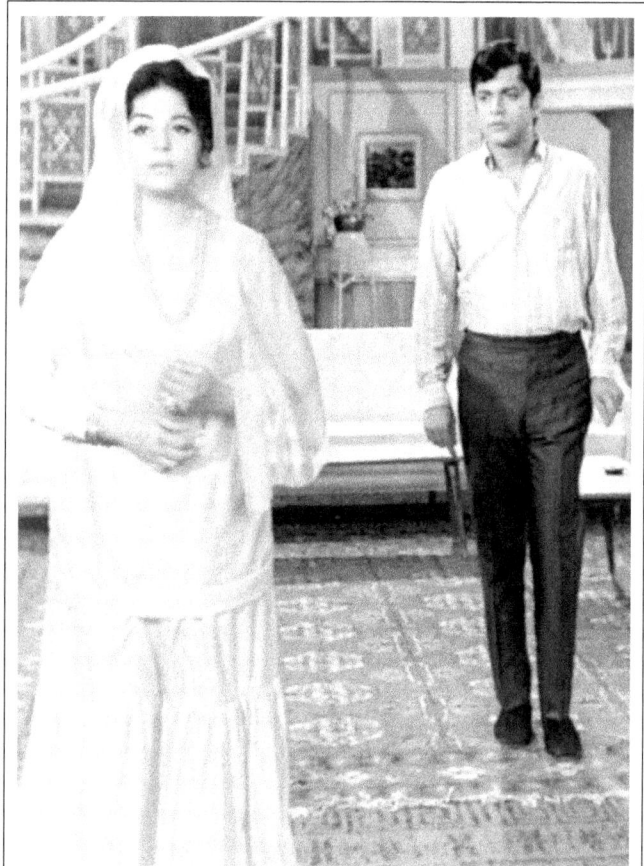

Waheed and Sabiha Khanam in *Anjuman*

---

[1] This has already been discussed in Chapters 1, 2 and 3.
[2] Interview in *Silver Jubilee* (1983), already quoted.

Roshan, his character in his third movie, *Mamta*, was different because of having a darker side. Other roles of the sinister type include good or bad burglars in *Ik Nagina, Afsana, Hill Station, Daulat Aur Duniya, Jaal, Jab Jab Phool Khiley, Parakh, Insaan Aur Shaitan, Ghairao* and *Hero;* and the cheating husband in *Bahen Bhai.*

Waheed in *Aurat Raj*

The ultimate was *Sheeshey Ka Ghar*, where Waheed played a complete villain.

Two characters deviating more than any others from the norm were the role-reversed male in *Aurat Raj* and the snake-turned-human in *Naag Aur Nagin.*

The latter was among his finest. The story was the remake of an earlier movie, *Nagin* (1959), based on a South Asian folklore according to which the king cobra ('sheesh naag') could assume human form after the age of hundred. In the movie, it was changed to one thousand years, increasing the symbolic value. The remake went far beyond the original and may be treated as a parable laced with motifs from the story of Genesis. Waheed's portrayal of a serpent-hero was mesmerizing. His character had only five lines to speak to his love interest (Rani). The rest was communicated between the lovers through eye contact only.

Waheed as a snake-turned-human in *Naag Aur Nagin*

His fourth movie as an actor was his own production, *Heera Aur Pather.*[1] Unlike some actors before and after him, he did not portray the uneducated person by becoming less than himself. He infused into these characters the regular charm and charisma of himself. They could be termed as 'romantic self-affirmation' on the part of the unschooled among the audience.

To posterity, they may serve as a useful resource for investigating the whole concept of 'the noble savage'.[2] *Heera Aur Pather* might be the best example.

Other instances include *Mastana Mahi, Pyar Hi Pyar, Waqt, Wahda, Joogi, Goonj Uthi Shehnai, Khuda Aur Mohabbat, Awaaz, Raja Ki Ayai Gi Barat* and *Hero.*

---

[1] Already discussed in Chapters 1 and 2.

[2] The French thinker Rousseau believed that human being is essentially good and peaceful, therefore his depiction of the pre-civilization individual is often called 'the noble savage', and to accept it is 'romantic self-affirmation': Ter Ellingson (2001), p.332. For Rousseau's depiction of the State of Nature, see 'The Second Discourse', included in Rousseau (2002), pp.69-148.

A fifth persona was the costume character. Carefully to be excluded from this category are movies where the alternative world is presented just in order to draw comparison with contemporary urban life, such as *Naag Muni* and *Dil Ruba*. Waheed's character in such movies would naturally fall more

Rani and Waheed in the titles roles in *Laila Majnu*

properly into one of the categories mentioned above. Secondly, the alternative society is not meant to present a self-contained environment whose ambience is to be experienced by the viewer without any external reference.

Proper examples would include stories set up completely in bygone eras, ethnic settings or fictitious subcultures: *Joshh, Jaag Utha Insan, Samandar, Laila Majnu, Ishq Mera Naa* (Punjabi), *Naag Aur Nagin* (already mentioned in another category) and *Zaib-un-Nisa*.

To this may also be added movies that were the Pakistani equivalents of the 'Muslim social movie'. Some famous examples of this genre among the Indian movies include *Pukar* (1939), *Khandan* (1942), *Najma* (1943), *Nek Perveen* (1946), *Mughal-e-Azam* (1960) and *Pakeezah* (1972). The genre had originated in India before 1947, but had continued to develop thereafter. In the Indian context it has been defined as a love story 'in which both the lead characters are Muslim and the film does not take up a socio-political issue' (and hence distinguishable from contemporary Indian movies such as *My Name Is Khan*).[1]

In the case of the Pakistani cinema, this category should typically include only those movies where the 'Muslim social' ambience prevailed over all other aspects, or some aspect of Muslim personal law played a major part in the story.

Waheed's first movie of this type was *Eid Mubarak*, followed soon afterwards by his own production, *Ehsaan*. Other examples include *Jan-e-Arzoo, Baharo Phhool Barsao, Deedar* and *Surrayya Bhopali*.

---

[1] See Shvetal Vyas (2011), pp.1-2.

A publicity still of *Eid Mubarak*

Out of these, *Deedar* deserves to be remembered as one of the finest 'Muslim social' movies ever produced on either side of the border. Perhaps unintentionally, influences from Shakespeare and Nezami Ganjavi come together in a remarkable unity to raise the subject of marriage and divorce to the level of an epic. The role of a young and influential Nawab (played by Shahid) in enforcing a truce between two noble families at the very beginning of the movie is starkly reminiscent of the opening scenes of *Romeo and Juliet*. The later role of the Nawab in standing between the lovers (Rani and Waheed Murad) seems like a motif taken from the legend of Shirin Farhad, immortalized by Nezami. The essential elements of Nawab culture of the recent past thus reach an epic scale in this story of stubborn patriarchs, repressed youth, oppressed women and self-restrained emotions all interacting within the confines of two rivaling households.

A poster of the movie *Deedar*

125

Songs are inseparable from the screen image of Waheed. An average Pakistani movie used to include eight to ten songs at the time when Waheed joined the trade. The number decreased in the late 1970s, as the songs became longer. The last production of Film Arts, *Hero,* had six songs.

Waheed was not given any song in his first movie, *Aulad.* In *Daaman,* his character danced to upbeat Western music. In *Mamta,* he got a proper duet, 'Yeh zindagi haseen hai'. Beginning with this, songs became an integral part of his screen image – especially after *Armaan,* where he took five songs, an unusually large number for a male actor. The image of 'the singing hero' would stay with him forever.

It has been generally accepted that he had a special gift for bringing a song to life with his performance. What has usually gone unnoticed is the extent to which the literary quality of those songs may have contributed to the magical effect.

Traditionally, a song – 'geet' – was meant to convey a sentiment in the simplest possible manner and was not supposed to express an excellence in verbal art or the depth of emotion. A typical example is the song attributed to Nawab Wajid Ali Shah of Lucknow, and later immortalized by K. L. Saigal, 'Babul mora nayher...'

In the 1920s, Hafeez Jallundhri pioneered a new type of poetry in Urdu – with a spillover effect on Hindi as well. Taking optimism from Iqbal and simplicity from Tagore, Hafeez introduced a style that was marked by amusing subjects, entertaining themes and simple expression. A typical example was his phenomenally popular poem, 'Abhi Tou Mien Jawan Hoon' ('Still I am Young').[1] Influence of this new style can be discerned not only among poets of high literature like Mira Ji, but also among poets who began to dominate mainstream South Asian cinema from the 1950s onward – Shakeel Badayuni,

---

[1] See Khurram Ali Shafique (2014), p.113

126

Qateel Shifai, Sahir Ludhianvi, Majrooh Sultanpuri, and others. As a result, film songs became the antithesis of the traditional tasteless form of 'geet'.

By the time Waheed appeared on the screen, a typical film song was nothing less than a short poem. It followed the rules of rhyme and meter, embodied the subtleties of poetry, and entertained the listener with apt metaphors and wordplay.

It would be a big mistake to categorize the songs of Waheed's movies as 'popular' in the same sense as the lines sung by Elvis Presley, Beatles and other 'pop' artists. In fact, the critically acclaimed poetry of that

Hafeez Jallundhri

period – the poems of Faiz, Ahmad Nadeem Qasmi, Parveen Shakir and others – may have had more in common with 'pop' (after all, high and popular cultures can be seen as two sides of the same coin, as discussed with reference to *Ishara* in the previous chapter).

The true cultural significance of the film poetry of Pakistan has yet to be appreciated. Centuries ago, when Rumi delivered a powerful message through poetry, he was followed by hundreds of poets who popularized his message across different cultures and languages through simple songs and poems, set to music for mass consumption. Today they are known as the folk heritage and the Sufi poetry of those cultures – Ameer Khusro, Fariduddin Masud Ganj Shakkar, Rahman Baba, Khushhal Khan Khattak, Bullhe Shah, Shah Abdul Latif Bhittai, Waris Shah, Sachal Sarmast, Ghulam Farid and many others.

Iqbal was also a phenomenon just like Rumi. He was also followed by a cluster of junior poets, beginning with Hafeez Jallundhri, Mian Bashir Ahmad, Hakeem Ahmed Shuja, Shakil Badayuni and many others in his own lifetime.

The poets who wrote songs for the movies of Waheed were doing for Iqbal the work which the folk and Sufi poets had done for Rumi in another age. They were taking the essence of Iqbal's message to the masses in the language of love and romance. The sentiments celebrated in these songs comprise of the virtues emphasized in Iqbal's poetry – idealism, love, healthy imagination, positive outlook on life, faith, patience and so on.

In his 125 movies, at least 319 songs featured Waheed as the singer.[1] Playback singers whose voices were used in these songs included (in the alphabetical order): A. Nayyar, Ahmad Rushdi, Akhlaq Ahmad, Ustad Amanat Ali Khan, Asad Amanat Ali, Bashir Ahmed, Ghulam Abbas, Ghulam Ali, Masood Rana, Mehboob Pervez, Mehdi Hassan, Mehnaz, Mujib Alam, Muneer Hussain, Rafiq Chaudhri, Rajab Ali, Safdar Javed, Saleem Raza and Salim Shahzad. To this list may also be added female singers Naheed Akhtar and Samar Iqbal, who lent their voices for the male-turned-female character of Waheed in *Aurat Raj*.

However, the voice that became inseparable from his screen image was that of Syed Ahmad Rushdi. He was born in the princely state of Hyderabad (Deccan) on April 24, 1934. His father Maulana Syed Manzoor Ahmad was a renowned scholar of hadis and a teacher of Arabic and Persian, and it is said that his pupils included Maulana Abul Ala Maududi. Unlike many ulema of the day, Syed Manzoor was a follower of the All-India Muslim League and an ardent supporter of the Pakistan movement.[2] He migrated to Karachi along with his family in 1954.

Rushdi's desire to make a career in music was understandably disliked by his family but one of the earliest assignments he got after arriving in the new state was the national anthem written by Hafeez Jallundhri, recorded that year for the first time. He was among the eleven singers who sang the anthem in chorus. The recording remained the only one to be used until the end of the century, and is the only authentic version to this date.

He also became famous with his children's song for the radio, 'Bunder Road se Kaemari', around the same time. He started playback singing in 1956 and acquired stardom with his 'Gol gappay wala aya' for the movie *Mehtab* in 1962. The phenomenal success of the song remains unprecedented – more than fifty years later it is still played by the vendors selling 'gol gappa', a popular street snack.

---

[1] List of songs retrieved on August 5, 2015 from
http://mazhar.dk/film/actors/WaheedMurad.php
[2] Absar Ahmed (2015)

L to R: Mala, Ahmad Rushdi, Waheed and Saeed A. Haroon

According to an unconfirmed estimate, he sang a total of 951 playback songs – more than any other playback singer in Pakistan. These included songs in Urdu (812), Punjabi (132), Sindhi (3) and English (1).[1] In 1969, he performed the largest number of playback songs by a male singer in a single year. Awards received during his lifetime included five Nigars (two for Waheed Murad songs, 'Akele na jana' in *Armaan* and 'Aye abr-e-karam' in *Naseeb Apna Apna*). Posthumous awards include a Nigar for Life Achievement in 2004 and Sitara-i-Imtiaz from the Government of Pakistan the same year.[2] He suffered three heart attacks, in 1976, 1981 and 1983. He had to retire from singing for some time due to this reason. The last song, which he recorded shortly before his death, was a patriotic song addressed to posterity. He died of his third heart attack on April 11, 1983.[3]

Waheed and Rushdi were the first Pakistani actor and singer respectively to have a hundred songs together.

---

[1] The source of this information is Mazhar Iqbal (Website). Retrieved on May 5, 2015, from http://mazhar.dk/film/artists/details.php?pid=191
[2] The source of this information is Wikipedia. Retrieved on May 5, 2015, from http://en.wikipedia.org/wiki/Ahmed_Rushdi
[3] Absar Ahmed (2015)

The Indian psychoanalyst Sudhir Kakar has tried to explain why certain types of character became popular in Indian cinema in the twentieth century. Although his study is restricted to the Indian movies, it may be interesting to use his observations as a checklist for the South Asian cinema in general.

Treating the popular cinema as 'a collective fantasy, a group daydream'[1], Kakar identifies three cultural prototypes that became prominent in the mainstream Indian cinema of the twentieth century.[2]

The first type has been named by him as Krishna-lover, after the legendary figure of Hindu mythology – also popular among Muslim artists and thinkers.[3]

Kakar finds reflections of the Krishna mythology in those male characters of the Indian cinema who express their masculinity through robust playfulness and bring out self-consciousness and modesty in a woman who was previously unaware of her femininity, and had confronted the hero boldly.[4]

Dev Anand and Shammi Kapoor have been named as the typical examples, but of course one could add many more – including the character played by Dilip Kumar in *Aan*.

In the case of Waheed, only a partial glimpse of this prototype may be seen – usually in the first halves of those movies where he portrays the role of a well-to-do young man (the second of his five 'personas' discussed earlier in

---

[1] Sudhir Kakar (1989/1990), p.26. He does not mean an expression of 'a mythic collective unconscious' or a group mind but 'that world of imagination which is fueled by desire and which provides us with an alternative world where we can continue our longstanding quarrel with reality.'

[2] Sudhir Kakar (1989/1990), pp.25-41. The theory of unconscious on which the psychoanalytic approach is ultimately based was questioned by Iqbal for its apparent lack of adequate evidence. The same line of argument appears to be the basis of the criticism by Ernest Gellner in our times. See Dr. Sir Muhamad Iqbal (1930/34), p.26; and Ernest Gellner (1985/2003), especially pp.65-69.

[3] Iqbal praised him as a forerunner of the philosophy of *khudi* and Hafeez Jallundhri wrote two odes to him.

[4] This type of heroine was more popular in the Pakistani cinema of the 1950s, epitomized by the character of Kausar (played by Sabiha Khanam) in *Saat Lakh* (1957). See Khurram Ali Shafique (1993a) and (1995b)

Waheed and Rani – possibly, a still from the lost movie, *Saaz-o-Awaz*

this chapter). Invariably, this character soon transforms into a different kind of personality – more introspective, sober and chastised.

This second personality is similar to what Kakar calls the Majnu hero – after the romantic lover immortalized by Nezami.[1] However, Kakar's description may not match the characters played by Waheed. According to Kakar, this type of character is a self-recriminating soul who 'must split off his corporeality and find it a home or, rather, an orphanage.'[2] One of the most enduring examples in the South Asian cinema has been Devdas, the hero of the classic Bengali novel successively portrayed by K. L. Saigal, Dilip Kumar and Shah Rukh Khan – and also by Habib in a Pakistani version produced in Dacca [Dhaka].

This is a far cry from the Majnu type of hero in Waheed's movies. Even his portrayal of the legendary Majnu – in Hassan Tariq's *Laila Majnu* – is not that of an absconder but rather someone who becomes stronger in hibernation and comes back to overturn the existing order of things.

---

[1] Regarding Indian cinema too, Kakar observed that 'the two, in a particular film, be sequential rather than separate.' Sudhir Kakar (1989/1990)
[2] Sudhir Kakar (1989/1990)

He may have to 'split off his corporeality', i.e. transcend the limitations of a physical existence and win the spirit a victory over matter. This he does not do by negating the self but rather by affirming it. At the end of *Armaan*, the characters of Nasir and Najma have grown so much larger than life that we can hardly expect them to meet in the mundane world where mortals like us live. This status is achieved by them, not by turning away from the physical world but by overcoming it.

The difference between the treatment of the Majnu type of hero in Indian cinema and the movies of Waheed has an analogy in the different attitudes towards personality in the two cultures.

Traditional Hinduism, like other pantheistic systems of thought, negates the ego – *khudi* – and aims at absorption in universal life. Modern Muslim thought is animated by the desire to discipline the ego and to immortalize it.

'The moral and religious ideal of man is not self-negation but self-affirmation,' says Iqbal. 'He attains to this ideal by becoming more and more individual, more and more unique … The greater his distance from God, the less his individuality. He who comes nearest to God is the completest person. Not that he is finally absorbed in God. On the contrary, he absorbs God into himself … by assimilating Divine attributes.'[1]

A similar difference may also be observed in the journeys of the heroines in both cases. If the Krishna-type lover in the Indian movies makes the female self-conscious, the same type of character in a Waheed Murad movie makes her self-aware.

One of most striking examples of the Krishna type of lover in the repertoire of Waheed is his character in *Tumhi Ho*

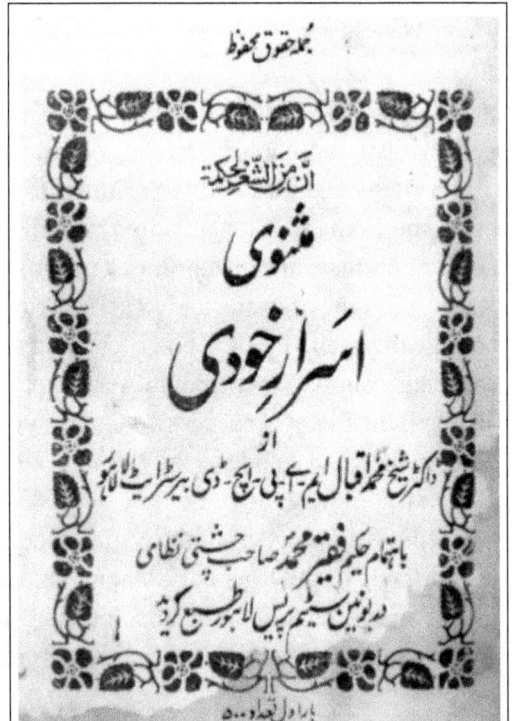

Cover of the first edition of Iqbal's 'Asrar-i-Khudi' (Secrets of the Self), 1915

---

[1] Dr. Sir Muhamad Iqbal (1978)

Mehboob Mere, who even claims in one of his songs, 'Mein hoon ashiq sadyoun purana, mien nay haseenoan ko naaz sikhaye' ('I am a centuries old lover; I have taught damsels how to be coquettish'). After interacting with this character, the heroine is led to a process of introspection that results in self-awareness – aptly described in the several songs attributed to her in the movie.

Nuri of *Heera Aur Pather* and Aalia of *Ishara* are two other examples of heroines becoming self-aware

Waheed and Deeba in *Jan-e-Arzoo*

through interaction with the hero. The most complete case studies are Jamila and Reshma in *Mastana Mahi.*

If Najma of *Armaan* may be considered the most representative heroine of the Waheed Murad movie, it may be said that the most typical heroine of a Waheed Murad movie is a self-aware and mature personality from the start. She is not particularly dependent on the hero for her self-discovery.

Kakar has also identified a third type of character that became popular in Indian cinema in the last quarter of the twentieth century. He has named this type Karna, after a character in the Sanskrit epic *Mahabharata,* who was deserted by his mother soon after birth. He later refused to listen to her when she tried to stop him from going to war against his brothers. There is an obvious resemblance between him and some of the most famous roles of Amitabh Bachan – including those in *Deewaar* (1975) and *Shakti* (1982).

Faint premonitions of this type could be found in the character of Waheed in *Daulat Aur Duniya.* His character in a later movie, *Ghairao,* was apparently inspired by the characters of Amitabh himself. Still, there is a difference that needs a little discussion.

Indian cinema after 1947 is perhaps unique in its admiration of characters who kill their blood-relations. Such acts can be found

Waheed in *Ghairao*

in literature of all times and regions, but elsewhere they are usually accompanied with remorse, penance and condemnation or retribution – the killing of father in the ancient Greek tragedy *Oedipus;* the slaying of a son in the classic Persian tale of Rostem and Sohrab; the murder of a brother in *Hamlet,* and so on. Wether the slaying is accidental or by design, it is met with horror and is heavily lamented. Invariably, it is treated as an act that disturbs the natural order of things, so that equilibrium needs to be regained by reversing the act whatever it takes – 'O cursèd spite, / That ever I was born to set it right!'

Not so in Indian cinema *after* 1947. There one finds a string of box office hits that offer moral and legal pretexts for eliminating a blood-relative. In *Mother India,* the heroine kills her son in order to prevent him from molesting a woman and gets identified with the motherland itself. In *Mughal-e-Azam,* an emperor exiles his would-be daughter-in-law and is thereby declared the saviour of the land. In *Gunga Jumna,* a brother kills brother. In *Deewaar,* a brother receives a medal for doing so. In *Shakti,* a father kills his son, and passes on the spirit to his grandson – the victim's son – as legacy.

Although it can be traced back to *Mahabharata* itself – a kind of the-Zen-of-killing-your-cousins – the extent to which the idea has obsessed the modern India is a phenomenon that deserves to be studied in detail.[1]

The theme could not sell in Pakistan. An odd exmaple is *Joshh,* where Waheed plays the role of a good son killing a bad father. The movie was not very successful – in spite of two memorable love songs.

---

[1] See Khurram Ali Shafique (2012b) for a study of the theme of fratricide in the Indian movie *Deewaar* (1975).

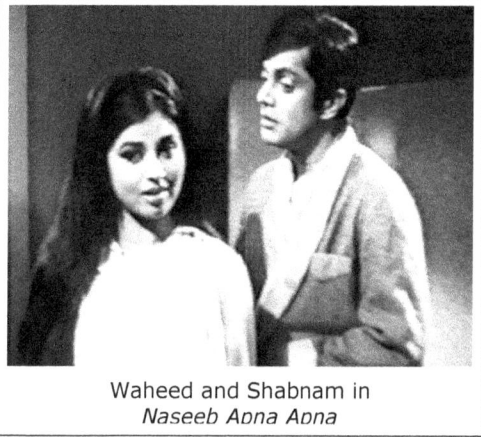

It has been suggested that Waheed became popular because the Pakistani society of the 1960s had escapist tendencies. It had become too complacent under the benevolent authoritarianism of General Ayub Khan, and the movies of Waheed offered escapism.

This point of view was presented in an article published in the magazine *Payami* (the Urdu

Waheed and Shabnam in
Naseeb Apna Apna

edition of *The UNESCO Courier* published by Hamdard Foundation, Karachi) sometime in 1985.[1] Taking cue from it, the present writer developed the thesis further through several articles written for the press between 1987 and 2006.[2]

On further analysis the thesis has turned out to be wrong about the cinema and its audience both. In the present book, it has already been shown that the society was anything but complacent at the time when Waheed became popular, and that his movies were relevant to the issues at hand.

It might be more fruitful to approach the subject from an evolutionary point of view, i.e. where society wants to go, and how far cinema has shown the way. The evolutionary approach has long been ignored by social scientists but some are turning back to it now.

'Culture is not causeless and disembodied,' it has been said. 'It is generated in rich and intricate ways by information-processing mechanisms situated in human minds. These mechanisms are, in turn, the elaborately sculpted product of the evolutionary process.'[3] Catching up with such trends may require revisiting a lesson the Pakistanis forgot long ago.

---

[1] The author read this article at that time but could not access the file now.
[2] See, e.g., Khurram Ali Shafique (1993a) and (1995b).
[3] Jerome H. Barkow, et. al. (Ed.; 1992/1995), p.3

135

More than a hundred years back, the American sociologist Franklin Henry Giddings proposed that the popularity of a character type in a society corresponds to the evolutionary needs of that society. The theory is still worth considering because it has a permanent place in the cultural history of Pakistan. It was used by Iqbal for determining the cultural and educational ideals of the South Asian Muslims in his paper 'The Muslim Community – a Sociological Study' (1911).

Franklin Henry Giddings

Giddings identified four types of character that may be discovered by a society in the course of its collective evolution.[1] He suggested:

1. THE FORCEFUL AND VALIANT TYPE is admired in primitive societies where the struggle for existence calls for such qualities.
2. THE CONVIVIAL TYPE replaces the previous one partially or completely, once the peril is over.
3. THE AUSTERE TYPE appears as a reaction against the excesses of the first two.
4. A RATIONALLY CONSCIENTIOUS TYPE appears only after a society has passed through all earlier stages of experience (this is essentially the austere type, now attempting to go beyond puritanical limitations).[2]

The type of character usually associated with Waheed is the third of these – the austere type, 'who can firmly put aside the pleasures of life, and in mere

---

[1] '...at a particular time, some one type of character is generally preferred. Consequently the prevailing ideal, then and there cherished, is that of a complete realization of the preferred character. The subordinate ideals are mental images of the economic, moral, and social conditions that are conceived to be necessary as means to the perfection of the ideal character.' Franklin Henry Giddings (1900/1901), p.317

[2] Franklin Henry Franklin Henry Giddings (1900/1901), pp.316-322; and (1900), pp.80-84

Waheed as Nasir in *Armaan*

duty give himself to severe employments.'[1] If Sohail Rana's description of the theme of *Armaan* (already quoted) is translated into the language of Giddings, it can be said that *Armaan* is about the metamorphosis of the convivial type of character into the austere type:

- Nasir starts as a prosperous and gifted person in whom accomplishment is combined with generosity, liberality of spirit, and the love of enjoyment. This is how Giddings describes the convivial type.[2]
- He gradually transforms into someone 'who holds up the ideal of self-control, and is dominated by a more serious view of life'. This is how Iqbal describes the austere type, based on the work of Giddings.[3]

The political, social and economic circumstances of Pakistani society around that time were also the same which, according to Giddings, create the demand for this type of character:

---

[1] Franklin Henry Giddings (1900/1901), p.319
[2] Franklin Henry Giddings (1900/1901), p.318
[3] Dr. Sir Muhammad Iqbal (1977/1995), p.127

Waheed, Rozina and Hanif in *Samandar*

Under circumstances of prolonged and general hardship, when the mere maintenance of life becomes difficult, this demand is strengthened by experiences of intolerable burdens laid upon the prudent by all extravagant indulgences on part of the reckless. Under such circumstances, the demand is not only for self-restraint, but also for self-denial. It is then that the austere man ... is idealized by thousands of those humble and patient ones to whom the struggle for existence has brought neither any great success nor overwhelming disaster, but only life itself, in exchange for unremitting toil.[1]

Giddings identifies two prominent trends in a community that favours chiefly the austere person: (a) it 'devotes itself to the establishment of civil justice'; or (b) it 'insists upon ceremonial purity, or upon ceremonial righteousness'.[2] In Waheed's society, both trends reached their peaks in his time. The political movements of the late 1960s demanded civil justice with more fervour than ever before or ever since. The agitation against Zulfikar Ali Bhutto in 1977 – coinciding with a similar zeal for Islamization in Bangladesh – revealed the desire for ceremonial purity and ceremonial righteousness, which the liberal regimes of both countries had overlooked.

---

[1] Franklin Henry Giddings (1900/1901), p.319
[2] Franklin Henry Giddings (1900/1901), p.321

Epilogue
The Answer

C an we find through our recent heritage the much-needed confidence in our existence as a people? Hopefully, the question may now be answered in the affirmative in light of what has been presented here. Regarding the austere type of character – the type associated with Waheed Murad – I wrote in *Iqbal: His Life and Our Times:*

> Iqbal upheld the austere type as 'the Muslim type of character' and proposed that all education in the Muslim community should aim at developing this type of character. Later on, he would propose the same aim for art and literature, and would offer a complete programme to this end in his first book of poetry, *Secrets and Mysteries.*[1]

The quest for this type of character and the desire to create a world suitable for it became the driving force for those who supported the All India Muslim League in the election of 1945-46, as shown in my previous book. The best description of their common goal may be found in the following words of the Quaid:

> What is it that you want? All this talk of socialism, communism, national-socialism and every other *ism* is out of place. Do you think you can do anything just now? How and when can you decide as to what form of government you are going to have in Pakistan? We are told by one party or another that we must have a democratic or a socialistic or a 'nationalistic' form of government in Pakistan. These questions are raised to hoodwink you. At present you should just

---

[1] Shafique (2014), p.70

Quaid-i-Azam Muhammad Ali Jinnah (1876-1948)

stand by Pakistan. It means that first of all you have to take possession of a territory. Pakistan cannot exist in the air. When you have once taken possession of your homelands the question will then arise as to what form of government you are going to establish. Therefore, do not allow your mind to be diverted by these extraneous ideas.[1]

Some of the intelligentsia allowed their minds to be diverted by these 'extraneous ideas'. Through some accident of history they happen to be the only ones whose voices have been taken seriously in Pakistan until now.

As a a result, very little is known about the perspective of those who stood by Pakistan just as the Quaid had advised, and through whom the evolution of the austere type of character was completed. The following sound bites may help us understand their point of view:

- Ibn-e-Safi devoted his life and work to a single message: 'Respect the law'. This was in line with the goal outlined by the Quaid.
- In 1996 – two years after he directed his last movie – I asked Pervez Malik why in spite of making so many movies about patriotic themes he never picked up issues like democracy and civil liberties in any of those movies. His answer was, 'Such issues are rather too advanced. They come later.'[2]
- As already mentioned, when I asked Javid Ali Khan, the childhood friend of Waheed, about the primary inspiration of Waheed, he said, 'We grew up with a mind to serve the nation just the way the Quaid-i-Azam and Quaid-i-Millat Liaquat Ali Khan had asked us to do. Waheed believed that he could do this through movies.'
- In early 2014, at a time when things looked unusually bleak for Pakistan, I asked Iqbal Rizvi – the writer of *Heera Aur Pather* and many other movies of Film Arts – if he still believed that Pakistan had a future. Rizvi answered in the affirmative. His argument was that three successive generations, of those who inhabited the land before 1947 and those who migrated later, have accepted it as their homeland.
- The same year, 2014, Sohail Rana was asked on a Canadian TV channel what he thought about the crisis in Pakistan and what should be done. His answer was that a troubled period of ten or twenty years means nothing in the life of a nation, and that bigger powers also went through

[1] Saleena Karim (2010), p.139
[2] Khurram Ali Shafique (1996b)

horrible times in their histories. What is to be done is that everybody should serve Pakistan with dedication. The solution, he said, was the motto given by the Quaid – faith, unity and discipline.

These are the people Waheed worked with. It should be obvious from the testimonials cited here that they devoted themselves to the cherished goal of the nation, just as the Quaid had described it. What other type of character could they have given us except the one that went together with that goal?

The evolution of the austere type of character in literature was evidently aided by its real world manifestation in the late 1930s. The Quaid was widely perceived by his followers as this type of character. One example is the poem 'Millat ka Pasban' ('The Defender of the Nation'), written by Iqbal's disciple Mian Bashir Ahmad and recited in the historic session of the All-India Muslim League at Lahore in March 1940.

Ever since then, the Quaid has occupied a pivotal position in the uniform culture of his people, explicitly as well as implicitly. Explicit references include the clever use of his photographs in movies like *Ishara* and *Jaal,* as already mentioned. In *Sachai* (1975), directed by Pervez Malik, the devotion of an honest civil servant to the deceased Father of the Nation is the central theme. One of the most touching references occurs in *Bhaiya* (1966), an Urdu movie from East Pakistan which featured Waheed in the lead role. In her moment of distress, the heroine (played by a Bengali talent) stands in front of a photograph of the Quaid and recalls him saying that he would rather not have a Pakistan where the poor continued to be exploited.[1] She then addresses his picture and says:

> We have not forgotten your message, Quaid. It has been forgotten by those wealthy ones, who think that the country is their private

---

[1] The lines are from the presidential address at the session of the All-India Muslim League at Delhi, on 24 April 1943: 'There are millions and millions of our people who hardly get one meal a day. Is this civilisation? Is this the aim of Pakistan? Do you visualise that millions have been exploited and cannot get a meal a day! If that is the idea of Pakistan, I would not have it.' Quoted in Saleena Karim (2010), p.146

property. They shatter our peace and comfort for the sake of their own pleasure. They destroy us, Oh my benefactor ... Today I rise against them ... so that I may prove that our Quaid is right. His word is true.

The movie was released in the same year when Mujib presented his Six Points. Implicitly, the Quaid served as the template for Col. Faridi, the hero of Ibn-e-Safi. The similarities between the two have been listed in one of my Urdu books, *Rana Palace* (2011). This should not be surprising because, as we have seen, they represented the same character type in history and fiction, respectively.

Likewise, Nasir of *Armaan* represents the same in cinema. The similarities between him and the Quaid are easy to notice if we turn to our leading anthropologist, Dr. Akbar S. Ahmed, for the most striking aspects of the popular image of the Quaid. According to him:

What continues to baffle people is the transformation of Jinnah from a liberal, Anglicized, seemingly secular politician ... into the champion of an exclusive Muslim identity.[1]

We only need to compare this with how Sohail Rana describes the transformation of Nasir in *Armaan:*

The point in *Armaan* is that it is the story of a young boy who is modern, and likes to go out to clubs ... As he matures through falling in love with a girl, he undergoes a reformation. Now he is not a visitor of the clubs; he does not take his beloved to the club, nor does he want such a girl as his beloved.[2]

The parallel is almost exact. The agent of change in the case of the Quaid is Muslim identity and in the case of Nasir it is Najma, and therefore Najma becomes the metaphor for the nation if the story is interpreted symbolically. The change in the wardrobe of Nasir – from the evening suit in 'Kokokorina' to the persistent use of kurta-pyjama in the latter part of the movie – also mirrors the change in the Quaid from his Sevile Row suits to the national dress.

Yet, a mere transformation from Western to native cannot be a big deal by itself. It was commonplace in the colonies ruled by European masters, and Gandhi is a much more striking example than anybody else. What was peculiar

---

[1] Akbar S. Ahmed (1997/2005), pp.66-67. He describes it as 'one of the most intriguing yet least explored areas of modern South Asian history.'
[2] Complete statement has been quoted in Chapter 3.

about the Quaid was the fact that he did not attempt to give an ideology to his people, nor asked them to follow *his* inner light. Instead, he ensured that they should get the right to choose whatever they wanted to, and he pledged himself to defending *their* ideology. In *Armaan*, Nasir also breaks the ice with Najma by asking her opinion on the subject of marriage. Incidentally, Najma's answer is not unlike the two-nation principle the Muslim community gave to the Quaid. 'The making and breaking of relationships is in the hand of God,' says Najma.

Such omnipresence of the Quaid in the collective imagination has also been pointed out by one of the foremost representatives of the cinematic literature. The poet Kaleem Usmani writes in one of his national songs:

ہے خون اُسی کا گرم سفر ہر راہِ وفا کے سینے میں

تصویر اُسی کی ہنستی ہے اِس بزم کے ہر آئینے میں

تعبیر کے سانچے میں جس نے ہر خواب کی صورت ڈھالی ہے

The lines can roughly be translated as: 'His blood it is that courses through all the paths of loyalty; his picture it is that smiles from every mirror in this gathering; he who has moulded every dream into the form of reality.'

This is the experience of those who traversed the paths of loyalty. As we know, those paths are uncharted territory for our authorities of art and literature, who have always been admittedly opposed to the common goal of the nation:

- On March 6, 1948, the stalwarts of the Progressive Literary Movement founded the Communist Party of Pakistan in Calcutta, India. Perceiving Pakistan to be a small and fragile country, the party hoped to bring about a 'revolution' that would push the country into the Soviet block. It was led by Faiz Ahmad Faiz, Sajjad Zaheer and others.
- They were opposed by Muhammad Hasan Askari, who also raised the slogan of 'Pakistani culture', but claimed that he was wiser than the

Quaid simply because he had read more books! Together with his disciples, such as Saleem Ahmad, he spent a lifetime demolishing the intellectual legacy of Iqbal, Hali and Sir Syed. This was done in the name of preserving 'tradition'. It is difficult to rationalize this type of mentality, so the less said about it the better.

- The novels usually described as the greatest in Urdu fiction are *Aag Ka Darya* (The River of Fire) by Quratul Ain Hyder and *Udas Naslayn* (Sad Generations) by Abdullah Husain. The first is a blunt rebuttal of the principle on which Pakistan was founded. The second presents an overview of Muslim society before the birth of Pakistan but portrays the masses as completely lacking in that will or intent which, according to the Quaid, had led to the birth of Pakistan.

- The spate of violence unleashed by Maula Jatt has already been discussed in Chapter 2. This notorious character was conceived by Ahmad Nadeem Qasmi, a representative of the Progressive Movement of Urdu literature.

It is commendable to tolerate dissenting voices. It is suicide to make them the sole criteria for judging a culture, and this is what we have been doing. This is why we have been living like a people who have collectively lost their memory and their sense of direction.

The dying wish of Waheed was that we should listen to a song from his movie, *Doraha*. The opening lines of the song are:

بھولی ہوئی ہوں داستاں، گزرا ہوا خیال ہوں

جس کو نہ تم سمجھ سکے میں ایسا اک سوال ہوں

The lines can roughly be translated as: 'I am a story forgotten. I am a thought deserted. I am a question you failed to understand.'

The story we have forgotten is the history of our ideals. Waheed is that story because he personified those ideals. The thought we have deserted is our cherished goal, and Waheed is its artistic representation. His life, work and even his death raise the question: *Can we find through our recent heritage the much-needed confidence in our existence as a people?* Our problem is not that we did not arrive at the correct answer. Our problem is that we could not understand the question.

Poster of a presentation by the author

Appendix 1
Awards
Received by Waheed Murad

1964
    Nigar Award, Best Actor for *Heera Aur Pather*

1965
    Rooman Award, Best Actor for *Eid Mubarak*

1966
    Nigar Award, Best Producer for *Armaan*
    Rooman Award, Best Actor for *Armaan*
    Rooman Award, Best Producer *for Armaan*
    Noor Jahan Award, Best Actor for *Armaan*
    Noor Jahan Award, Best Producer for *Armaan*

1967
    Shabab Award, Best Actor for *Insaniyat*

1969
    Nigar Award, Best Actor for *Andaleeb*
    Rooman Award, Best Actor for *Andaleeb*
    Graduate Award, Best Actor for *Andaleeb*
    Chitrali Award, Best Actor for *Andaleeb*
    Khlail Qaiser Award, Best Actor for *Andaleeb*
    Curtex Award, Best Actor for *Andaleeb*

1971
    Nigar Award, Best Actor (Punjabi) for *Mastana Mahi*
    Graduate Award, Best Actor (Punjabi) for *Mastana Mahi*

1974

Rooman Award, Best Actor for *Phool Mere Gulshan Ka*

1975

Graduate Award, Best Actor for *Jab Jab Phool Khiley*
Mussawir Award, Best Actor for *Jab Jab Phool Khiley*
Sindh Awami Award, Best Actor for *Jab Jab Phool Khiley*
Aghaz Award, Best Actor for *Jab Jab Phool Khiley*

1976

Sindh Awami Award, Best Actor for *Shabana*

1978

PIA Academy Award, Best Actor for *Awaaz*
Al-Fankar Award, Best Actor for *Awaaz*
Chaministan International Award for Public Popularity Competition, Most
Popular Film Star

1979

PIA Academy Award, Best Actor for *Bahen Bhai*
National Award, Best Actor for *Bahen Bhai*

1980

Al-Fankar Award, Best Actor for *Badnaam*

1981

Riaz Shahid Award, Best Actor for *Ghairao*

1982

National Academy Award, Best Supporting Actor for *Aahat*

1983

Mussawir Award, Lifetime Achievement Award

1985

Shabab Memorial Award, Best Supporting Actor for *Anokha Daaj* (1981)

2002

Nigar Award, Legend Award for Lifetime achievement

2011

Sitara-e-Imtiaz, Lifetime achievement

Appendix 2
FILMOGRAPHY

This is a complete list of 125 movies in which Waheed Murad appeared as an actor. Excluded from the list are his uncredited cameo appearances in *Sathi* (1959); and credited cameos in *Khushiya* (1973) and *Ajj Di Taza Khabar* (1978). The cumulative weeks (followed in brackets by consecutive weeks in the main theatre) are according to the Karachi Circuit, and have been taken from the website www.mazhar.dk, which is also the source of information for the release dates of the movies.

Alphabetical

Aadmi. Screenplay & Directed by M. A. Rasheed. Produced by Lala Abdul Aziz. Music: Kamal Ahmad. Lyrics: Qateel Shifai, Masroor Anwar, Saeed Gilani. Story: Anwar Batalvi. Dialogue: Rasheed Sajid. Cast: Muhammad Ali, Waheed Murad, Sangeeta, Kaveeta, Nisho, Lehri, Adeeb, Aslam Pervez, Talish, Kamal Irani, Ibrahim Nafis, Meena Dawood, Talat Siddiqui, Khalid Salim Mota, Surayya Khan, Iqbal Bukhari, Banka, Pani Walker, Sajjan, Najib, Dadu, Ghauri. 28 (3) Weeks. February 10, 1978

Aahat. Directed by Muhammad Javaid Fazil. Produced by Atta Buzdar. Music: Robin Ghosh. Lyrics: Saeed Gilani. Written by Syed Noor. Cast: Nadeem, Shabnam, Waheed Murad, Talish, Nannha, Ilyas Kashmiri, Najma Mehboob, Bindya, Roomana, Jamil Fakhri, Saqi, Anwar Ali, Ali Ahmed, Mirza Ghazanfar, Arslan, Aman Sufi, Ejaz Akhtar, Faisal Iqbal. 28 (3) Weeks. April 16, 1982

Aap Ka Khadim. Directed by Wazir Ali. Produced by Waqar Ali & Imtiaz Ali. Music: Khalil Ahmad. Lyrics: Taslim Fazli & Ratan Kumar. Written by Agha Hasan Imtisal. Cast: Muhammad Ali, Zeba, Waheed Murad, Azad, Hanif, Rangila, Najma, Afzal Ahmad, Bahar, Farzana, Tamanna, Shahnawaz, Ilyas Kashmiri, Masood Akhtar, Ibrahim Nafis, Asifa, . 25 (3) Weeks. March 12, 1976

Afsana. Directed by Luqman. Produced by Asghar Ali Bandookwala. Music: Nashad. Lyrics: Tanveer Naqvi & Taslim Fazli. Story, Screenplay & Dialogue: Dr. Anwer Sajjad. Cast: Deeba, Waheed Murad, Rozina, Nannha, Adeeb, Kamal Irani, Shakir. B&W. 28 (6). February 6, 1970

Afshan. Story & Direction: Javed Hashmi. Produced by Mohammed Ali. Music: Nashad. Lyrics: Taslim Fazli. Dialogue: Iqbal Rizvi. Cast: Waheed Murad, Shabnam, Aaliya, Lehri, Tariq Aziz, Saiqa, Muhammad Yusuf, Latif Charlie, S. M. Saleem, Naz Begum, Agha Jan, Tamanna, Sangeeta, Pundit Shahid, Zoni, Jami, Mushtaq Mirza, Habib-ur-Rehman, Anila Nafees, Farida Anjum, Shaista, Shaheen, Nighat Sultana, Nihal, Naurina, Chandni. 21 (5) Weeks. March 12, 1971

Akh Lari Bado Badi (Punjabi). Directed by Shafique Akhtar. Produced by Malik Feroz Din. Music: Master Abdullah. Written by Hazin Qadri. Lyrics: Hazin Qadri, Ahmad Rahi, Khwaja Pervez, Hafeez Suhail. Cast: Mumtaz, Waheed Murad, Munawar Zarif, Mustafa Qureshi, Alla-ud-din, Najma Mehboob, Ilyas Kashmiri, Adeeb, Nimmo, Nazli, Zarqa, Khalid Salim Mota, Aurangzeb, Changezi, Ladla, Chabela, Imdad Husain, . 16 (2) Weeks. September 26, 1976

Andaleeb. Directed by Fareed Ahmed. Screenplay & Produced by Rashid Mukhtar. Music: Nisar Bazmi. Lyrics: Kaleem Usmani. Story: Salma Kanwal. Dialogue: A. S. Afaqi. Cast: Shabnam, Waheed Murad, Talish, Aaliya, Mustafa Qureshi, Salma Mumtaz, Ibrahim Nafis, Baby Durdana, Atiya Sharaf, Talat Siddiqui, Rajni, Pandit Shahid, Sultana Iqbal, Khushtar, Meena Chaudhry. 56 (20) Weeks. August 29, 1969

Anhoni. Directed by Iqbal Akhtar. Produced by Qadeer Khan. Music: Lal Muhammad Iqbal. Script: Danish Dervi (based on the story of 'Anastasia'). Lyrics: Dukhi Premnagri. Cast: Waheed Murad, Aaliya, Zarqa, Lehri, Saqi, Rashid, Jalil Afghani, Seema, Sajan, Zahid Khan, Naz Begum. 31 (4) Weeks. December 21, 1973

Anjuman. Screenplay & Directed by Hassan Tariq. Produced by: Safdar Masud & Hassan Tariq. Music: Nisar Bazmi. Lyrics: Saifuddin Saif, Masroor

Anwar, Fayyaz Hashmi & Saroor Bara Bankavi. Story & Dialogue: Agha Hasan Imtisal. Cast: Rani, Waheed Murad, Deeba, Santosh, Sabiha Khanum Lehri, Tamanna, Ilyas Kashmiri, Gotam, Naizr Bedi, Dadoo, Mohsin. 81 (32) Weeks. July 31, 1970

Anokha Daaj (Punjabi). Directed by Aslam Dar. Produced by Aslam Dar & Qamar Butt. Music: Master Rafique. Lyrics: Waris Ludhianvi. Story & Dialogue: Sheikh Iqbal Cast: Sultan Rahi, Aasiya, Durdana Rehman, Waheed Murad, Sabiha Khanum, Ilyas Kashmiri, Tani, Sheikh Iqbal, Nasrullah Butt, Rehan, Saqi, Altaf Khan, Shehla Gil, Khawar Butt, Manzoora, Mustafa, Mochha, Rafique, Jabroo, Salim Khan, Banka, Mukhtar, Billa, Irshad, Sattar, Masood, Doctor, Kausar. 16 (3) Weeks. February 27, 1981

Apney Huay Paraey. Directed by Iqbal Akhtar. Produced by Riaz Bukhari & Muhammad Shafi. Music: M. Ashraf. Screenplay, Dialogue and Lyrics: Masroor Anwar. Story: Zahida Masroor. Cast: Mumtaz, Waheed Murad, Muhammad Ali, Sangeeta, Ghulam Mohi-ud-din, Nayyar Sultana, Qavi, Tamanna, Najma Mehboob, Nasira, Masood Akhtar, Kamal Irani, Gulnar, Agha Faraz, Maqbool, Mehbub Alam, Chakram, Aisha, Khalid Salim Mota, K. Kumar, Mirza Shahi, Tabassum. 32 (6) Weeks. December 2, 1977

Armaan. Screenplay & Directed by Pervez Malik. Written & Produced by Waheed Murad. Music: Sohail Rana. Lyrics & Dialogue: Masroor Anwar. Cast: Zeba, Waheed Murad, Tarranum, Nirala, Rozina, Bibbo, Zahoor Ahmad, Ansari, Qamar, Neelofar, Khurshid Kanwal, Rauf, Sharafat, Agha Sarwar (Debut). B&W. 76 (34) Weeks. March 18, 1966

Aulad. Directed by S. M. Yusuf. Produced by F. M. Sardar & S. M. Yusuf. Music: A. Hameed. Lyrics & Written by Fayyaz Hashmi. Cast: Nayyar Sultana, Habib, Talish, Waheed Murad (debut), Mumtaz Bukhari (debut), Lehri, Faizy, S. Gul, Salma Mumtaz, Sikandar, Jaffry, Saqi, G. N. Butt, Agha Jan, Raziya, Abushah, Bela Malik; Child stars: Aziz Yusuf, Shaukat Yusuf, Satish Anand, Pappu. B&W. 57 (32) Weeks. August 10, 1962

Aurat Raj. Written, Produced & Directed by Rangila. Music: Nazir Ali, M. Ashraf, Chandar Mohan, Beli Ram, Rangila. Lyrics: Taslim Fazli, Khwaja Pervez, Ahmed Shakil, Azim Malik, Rangila, Based on a central idea by Shaukat Thanvi. Cast: Waheed Murad, Rani, Sultan Rahi, Rangila, Chakori, Naghma, Badar Munir, Usman Pirzada, Asif Khan, Rangila, Qavi, Kamal Irani, Nannha, Ali Ejaz, Saqi, Shahnawaz, Yusuf Khan, Irfan Khoosat, Durdana, Albela, Khalid Salim Mota, Yasmin Khan, Chakram, Dimpel,

Sundra, Saira, Shehla Gil, Khanum, Waheed Khan, Suriya Khan, Iqbal Durrani, Ali Ahmad, Ladla, Bokhari, Nazar, Azam Jahangir, Zubair, Munna, Majid Shaukat, Zahid Khan. Child star Rehman. 45 (9) Weeks. July 13, 1979

Awaaz. Produced & Directed by Zafar Shabab. Music: A. Hameed. Story & Screenplay: Shabab Kairanvi. Dialogue: Riaz-ur-Rehman Saghar. Lyrics: Shabab Kairanvi, Qateel Shifai, Saeed Gilani. Cast: Muhammad Ali, Shabnam, Waheed Murad, Ghulam Mohi-ud-din, Nannha, Tamanna, Naghma, Bindya, Fozia Durrani, Masood Akhtar, Ibrahim Nafis, Afshan, Saqi, Badi-uz-Zaman, Chandni, Akhtar Shad, Riaz Shoqi, Zafar Fiaz, Majeed Shah, Musarrat. Child stars: Noreen, Anila, Guddu. 93 (10) Weeks. October 27, 1978

Badnaam. Directed by Iqbal Yusuf. Produced by Mian Muhammad Arshad. Music: Nashad. Lyrics: Taslim Fazli. Screenplay & Dialogue: Riaz Arshad. Cast: Muhammad Ali, Rani, Babra Sharif, Waheed Murad, Naghma, Habib, Lehri, Adeeb, Changezi, Akhter Shad, Ayub Khan, Chaudhry Iqbal, Erum, Pundit Shahid, Albela, Khalid, Kiran, Munna, Ilyas Anjum, Pervez, Kabliwala, Mehmood Khan, Tariq, Nishat Anjum, Majeed, . 41 (8) Weeks. October 3, 1980

Baharo Phool Barsao. Written & Directed by M. Sadiq (with contribution from Hassan Tariq)[1]. Produced by Mahmood Sadiq. Music: Nashad. Lyrics: Shevan Rizvi. Cast: Rani, Waheed Murad, Sangeeta, Rukhsana, Aslam Pervez, Munawar Zarif, Ilyas Kashmiri, Saiqa, Kamal Irani, Sh. Iqbal, Rehma, Abbas Nosha, Changezi, Nusrat Ara, Imdad Hussain, Musarrat Khan, Nazir Bedi, Naz Begum. 64 (23) Weeks. August 11, 1972

Bahen Bhai. Directed by Nazar Shabab. Produced by A. Hamid. Music: Kamal Ahmad. Lyrics: Qateel Shifai, Saeed Gilani. Story & Screenplay: Shabab Kairanvi. Dialogue: Basheer Niaz. Cast: Muhammad Ali, Rani, Waheed Murad, Sabiha Khanum, Nannha, Tamanna, Hanif, Ali Ejaz, Rangila, Saqi, Ibrahim Nafis, Bindya, Shahnawaz, Chakram, Inayat Anjum, Anwar Ali, Zameer Abser. Child stars: Baby Nadia, Master Nadeem. 52 (10) Weeks. January 19, 1979

Bahu Begum. Directed by Wazir Ali. Produced by A. M. Mirza. Music: Tassaduq. Lyrics: Musheer Kazmi. Story & Screenplay: Ijaz Akhtar. Dialogue: Arsh Lucknavi[2]. Cast: Deeba, Sabira Sultana, Nasira, Zeenat,

---

[1] Hassan Tariq contributed after Sadiq passed away before completing the movie.
[2] Spelled here as Lucknowi.

Habib, Waheed Murad, Saqi, Roshan, Nabila, Zammurad. B&W. 13 (5) Weeks. March 2, 1965

Bandagi. Directed by Fareed Ahmed. Produced by Saleem Ashrafi. Music: Nashad. Lyrics: Kaleem Usmani. Screenplay: A. S. Afaqi & Fareed Ahmed. Dialogue: A. S. Afaqi. Cast: Waheed Murad, Shabnam, S. M. Saleem, Talish, Santosh Russell, Talat Hussain, Farah Jalal, Hijab, Baby Nafisa, Zareen, Aamir Effendi, Aslam Raj, Shakoor Ishrat, Akhtar Khurram, Shaffan, G. R. Ashrafi, Siddique. 21 (4) Weeks. June 23, 1972

Bandhan. Directed by Aquil Pervez & Shaukat Hashmi. Produced by Raja S. Akhtar. Music: M. Ashraf. Lyrics: Akhter Yousuf. Written by Masood Mashhadi. Cast: Waheed Murad, Neelam, Najma, Ghulam Mohi-ud-din, Aslam Pervez, Kamal Irani, Hanif, Alia, Fozia Durrani, Lehri, Khalid Salim Mota, Mizla, Meena Dawood, Kashif Raja (debut), Shabo, Pani Walker, Ladan . 18 (2) Weeks. March 21, 1980

Be Wafa. Directed by S. Suleman. Produced by Irfan Malik. Music: Nisar Bazmi. Lyrics: Masroor Anwar, Kaleem Usmani & Taslim Fazli. Written by Agha Hasan Imtisal. Cast: Shamim Ara, Waheed Murad, Tamanna, S. M. Saleem, Saqi, Rangila, Mustafa Qureshi, Khalid Saeed Butt, Nabila, Rehana Siddiqui, Seema, Rajni, Chham Chham. B&W. 26 (4) Weeks. March 20, 1970

Bhaiya. Directed by Kazi Zahir. Produced by Sajida Anis Dossani. Music: Robin Ghosh. Lyrics: Ishrat Kalkatvi, Shaeer Siddique, Khauaja Rewaj. Screenplay: Arham Siddiky. Story: Najmul Alam. Dialogue: Shaeer Siddique. Cast: Chitra Singha, Waheed Murad, Shawkat Akbar, Anwar Hossain, Siraj Hossain, Ahmadur Rahman, Subhash Datta, Kazi Khaleque, Jalil Afgani, Mesbahuddin, Aktar Hossain, Fatty Mohsin, Badruddin, K. Kumar, Maska, Rashed, Master Badal. B&W. 39 (20) Weeks. October 14, 1966

Chand Suraj. Directed by Shore Lakhnavi. Produced by Ghulam Nasir Khan. Music: Nashad. Lyrics: Shore Lakhnavi, Shevan Rizvi, Moin Ahsan Jazbi. Cast: Rozina, Waheed Murad, Shabana, Nadeem, Kamal Irani, Sabira Sultana, Nannha, Najma, Tamanna, Hanif, Muhammad Yusuf, Ghulam Farid Sabri Qawwal, Maqbool Sabri Qawwal. 25 (2) Weeks. December 25, 1970

Chotee Nawab. Directed by Iqbal Akhtar. Produced by Begum Ahad Malik. Music: Nazir Ali. Lyrics: Taslim Fazli, Khwaja Pervez. Written by Agha Hasan Imtisal. Cast: Babra Sharif, Shahid, Waheed Murad, Neelo, Bindya,

Nannha, Shahnawaz, Ibrahim Nafis, Saqi, Farzana, Kamal Irani, Najma Mehboob, Masood Akhtar, Imrozia, Asifa, Hanif, Roomana, Mehboob Alam, Khalid Saleem Mota, Ladla, Abu Shah, Agha Faraz, Wasee Ahmad, Pervez Khan, Tariq Khan, Atique, Chakram, Mirza Shahi, Achhi Khan. 25 (2) Weeks. March 14, 1980

Daaman. Directed by Qadeer Ghauri. Produced by Santosh Kumar. Music: Khalil Ahmad. Lyrics by Himayat Ali Shair. Writtem by Hasrat Lucknavi. Cast: Sabiha Khanum, Santosh Kumar, Neelo, Lehri, Waheed Murad, Talish, Azad, Saqi, Aslam Pervez, Rajni, Tarana, Laddan, Jaffry. B&W. 69 (29) Weeks. May 13, 1963

Daulat Aur Duniya. Directed by Khalifa Saeed Ahmad. Produced by Khalida Khurshid Ahmed & Sarwar Saeed. Music: Kamal Ahmad. Lyrics: Tanveer Naqvi, Khwaja Pervez. Story Dialogue: Tanvir Kazmi. Dialogue, Court & Comedy Scenes: Sikkaidar. Cast: Waheed Murad, Rozina, Aaliya, Khalifa Nazeer, Nannha, Aslam Pervez, Zerqa, Afzaal Ahmad, Munawar Saeed, Shakil, Seema Sikkidar, Asif Naz, Mureed, Tahira Khatana, Naz Begum, . 46 (11) Weeks. April 28, 1972

Deedar. Screenplay & Directed by Hassan Tariq. Produced by Rabia Hassan. Music: Nashad. Lyrics: Saifuddin Saif. Written by M. Sadiq (late). Cast: Waheed Murad, Shahid, Rani, Mumtaz, Nayyar Sultana, Darpan, Talish, Alla-ud-din, Sabiha Khanum, Sangeeta, Nannha, Saqi, Tamanna, Meena Dawood, Asifa, Chhabela. 26 (6) Weeks. 62 (2) Weeks. November 15, 1974

Dewar Bhabhi. Directed by Hassan Tariq. Produced by: Santosh Kumar. Music: Master Inayat Hussain. Lyrics: Fayyaz Hashmi. Story: Arsh Lucknavi. Dialogue: A. S. Afaqi. Cast: Sabiha Khanum (credited as Sabiha Raza), Santosh Kumar, Waheed Murad, Rani, Lehri, Jaffry, Baby Najmi, Gotam. B&W. 55 (19) Weeks. May 5, 1967

Dil Mera Dharkan Teri. Screenplay & Directed by M. A. Rasheed. Produced by Mian Ghulam Murtaza Aftab & M. A. Rasheed. Music: Master Inayat Hussain. Lyrics: Qateel Shifai. Story: Mian Ghulam Murtaza Aftab. Dialogue: Masroor Anwar. Cast: Shamim Ara, Waheed Murad, Rani, Lehri, Talish, Chham Chham, Asad, Changaizi, Shakeel, Nighat Sultana, Salma Mumtaz, Sahira. B&W. 58 (18) Weeks. April 26, 1968

Dil Ney Phir Yaad Kiya. Directed by Iqbal Akhtar. Produced by Muhammad Naseem. Music: Kamal Ahmad. Lyrics: Taslim Fazli, Riaz-ur-Rehman Saghar. Written by Bashir Niaz. Cast: Babra Sharif, Shahid, Waheed Murad, Nayyar Sultana, Talish, Kamal Irani, Ibrahim Nafis, Mizla, Khalid Salim

Mota, Farzana, Chakram, Rashid, Ejaz, Mohsan, Boby. Child star: Imran Adnan. 45 (11) Weeks. May 15, 1981

Dil Ruba. Directed by Hassan Tariq. Produced by Habib-ul- Hassan. Music: M. Ashraf. Lyrics: Taslim Fazli. Story: Sheikh Iqbal. Screenplay & Dialogue: B. H. Bokhari. Cast: Rani, Waheed Murad, Husna, Nayyar Sultana, Bahar, Talish, Alla-ud-din, Mustafa Qureshi, Nirala, Waheeda Khan, Saqi, Khalid Salim Mota, Sheikh Iqbal, Pani Walker, Abu Shah, Mushtaq, Laddan, Ladla, . 24 (1 ½) Weeks. October 7, 1975

Doctor. Directed by Shaukat Hashmi. Music by Moslehuddin. Cast: Bahar, Waheed Murad, Yasmin, Jafri. B&W. 10 (2) Weeks. March 12, 1965

Doraha. Screenplay & Direction by Pervez Malik. Produced by Pervez Malik & Sohail Rana. Music: Sohail Rana. Lyrics & Dialogue: Masroor Anwar. Story: Syed Ahmad Rifat. Cast: Shamim Ara, Waheed Murad, Deeba, Talish, Nirala, Talat Siddiqui, Ibrahim Nafis, Mahmood Ali, Qurban Jilani, Latif Charlie, S. M. Saleem, Baby Jugnu, Badar Munir (uncredited), Hassan Pahari, Khurshid Kanwal, Ansari. B&W. 40 (7) Weeks. August 25, 1967

Dushman. Directed by Pervez Malik. Produced by Anis Dossani. Music: Nisar Bazmi. Lyrics: Masroor Anwar. Cast: Muhammad Ali, Waheed Murad, Mumtaz, Zeba, Adeeb, Atiya Sharaf, Nirala, Afzal Ahmad. 54 (15) Weeks. November 8, 1974

Ehsaan. Directed by Pervez Malik. Produced by Waheed Murad. Music: Sohail Rana. Lyrics, Story & Dialogue: Masroor Anwar. Cast: Waheed Murad, Zeba, Rozina, Nirala, Azad, Ibrahim Nafis, S. M. Saleem, Hasan Pahari, Latif Charlie, Khurshied Kanwal, Naseeruddin, Baby Jugnu, Mahmood Ali, Qazi Wajid, Zahoor Ahmad, Agha Sarwar, Fantosh, Ansari. B&W. 40 (12). June 30, 1967

Eid Mubarak. Directed by S. M. Yusuf. Produced by F. M. Sardar & S. M. Yusuf. Music: A. Hameed. Story, Dialogue & Lyrics: Fayyaz Hashmi. Cast: Zeba, Waheed Murad, Habib, Iqbal Yusuf, Nirala, Adeeb, Sabira Sultana, Seema, G.N. Butt, Kamal Irani, Faizy, Qamar. B&W. 40 (13) Weeks. July 2, 1965

Ek Nagina. Directed by Syed Ali Hafiz. Produced by Liaquat Gul Agha. Music: Amjad Hussain. Lyrics: Taslim Fazli. Written by Hasrat Lucknavi. Cast: Waheed Murad, Deeba, Lehri, Adeeb, Jaffry, S. M. Saleem, Aaliya, Zeenat, Saiqa, Tani, Saqi. B&W. 29 (6). September 9, 1969

Ghairao. Directed by Iqbal Yusuf. Produced by M. Sharif Siddiqui. Music: Tafooo. Story, Screenplay & Dialogue: Khurshidullah. Cast: Shabnum,

Mohammad Ali, Waheed Murad, Nayyar Sultana, Hanif, Asif Khan, Adeeb, Asif Raza Mir, Khalid Salim Mota, Albela, Changezi. 33 (5) Weeks. October 9, 1981

Goonj Uthi Shehnai. Directed by S. M. Yusuf. Produced by Muhammad Ashiq Butt. Music: M. Ashraf. Lyrics: Taslim Fazli. Written by Athar Shah Khan. Cast: Zeba, Muhammad Ali, Waheed Murad, Roohi Bano, Aslam Pervez, Kamal Irani, Meena Dawood, Ibrahim Nafis, Albela. 39 (6) Weeks. November 19, 1976

Gunman. Directed by Iqbal Yusuf. Produced by S. M. Yusuf. Music: Tafoo. Cast: Babra Sharif, Mohammad Ali, Waheed Murad, Mumtaz, Rani, Naghma, Adeeb, Hanif, Asif Khan, Khalid Salim Mota, Meena Dawood, Albela, Ishrat Chaudhry, Seema, Saqi . 32 (4) Weeks. May 8, 1981

Haqeeqat. Directed by Nazrul Islam. Produced by Saeeda Khan. Music: A. Hameed. Lyrics: Khwaja Pervez. Screenplay & Dialogue: Bashir Niaz. Cast: Muhammad Ali, Waheed Murad, Deeba, Babra Sharif, Talish, Adeeb, Tamanna, Nirala, Atiya Sharaf, Nasira, Khalid Nizami, Jalil Afghani, Rashid, Taj Multani, Arslan. 39 (10). November 1, 1974

Heera Aur Pather. Directed by Pervez Malik. Produced by Waheed Murad. Music: Sohail Rana. Lyrics: Masroor Anwar, Mauj Lakhnavi. Writtem by Iqbal Hussain Rizvi. Cast: Waheed Murad, Zeba, Kamal Irani, Ibrahim Nafis, Adeeb, Kammo, Nimo, Adeeb, Nirala, Agha Jan. B&W. 56 (25) Weeks. December 11, 1964

Hero. Directed by Iqbal Yusuf. Written & Produced by Waheed Murad. Music: Kamal Ahmad. Lyrics: Khwaja Pervez & Taslim Fazli. Cast: Waheed Murad, Babra Sharif, Mumtaz, Munawar Saeed, Tani, Huma Dar, Seema, Saqi, Adil Murad (debut), Khalid Saleem, Chakram, Hanif, Jahangir Moghul, Ashraf Chitta, Zaman, Rafiq Sindhi, Mustafa, Arshad Baig; Special appearances by Nadeem, Talish, Lehri, Aslam Pervez, Ilyas Kashmiri, Shahid, Ali Ejaz. 35 (5) Weeks. January 11, 1985

Hill Station. Directed & Produced by Iqbal Yusuf. Music: Nashad. Story & Songs: Taslim Fazli. Cast: Shamim Ara, Waheed Murad, Iqbal Yusuf, Mahpara, Hanif, Santosh Russell, Nirala, Azad, Chun Chun, Faizy, Aftab Sethi, Mahmood, Gulzar, Zareena, Zahid Shiraz (debut). 16 (3) Weeks. March 10, 1972

Honhaar. Directed by S. M. Yusuf. Produced by F. M. Sardar & S. M. Yusuf. Music: A. Hameed. Lyrics: Fayyaz Hashmi. Cast: Rukhsana, Waheed Murad, Shakeel (debut), Trannum, Kamal Irani, Rashid, Seema, Faizy,

Zahoor Ahmad, Saajan, Abbas Ajmeri. B&W. 12 (4) Weeks. March 25, 1966

I Love You. Screenplay & Directed by Jamshed Naqvi. Produced by Ch. Ghulam Sarwar Jaura. Music: M. Ashraf. Lyrics: Taslim Fazli, Masroor Anwar, Khwaja Pervez. Story based on a central idea by Munawar Shehzad, M.A. Dialogue: Syed Noor. Cast: Shabnam, Waheed Murad, Shahid, Nayyar Sultana, Aslam Pervez, Arzoo, Nannha, Shehla Gil, Jamshed Ansari, Tamanna, Khalid Salim Mota, Khalid Akhtar, Asifa, Chakram, Mustafa, Ali Ahmad, Tabassum. 27 (3) Weeks. March 12, 1982

Insaan Aur Shaitan. Directed by Khalifa Saeed. Produced by Khalifa Nazeer. Music: Kamal Ahmad. Cast: Waheed Murad, Shahid, Najma, Talish, Asif Khan, Nannha, Saiqa, Khalifa Nazeer, Asifa, Farah Jalal, Nasrullah, Nazli, Najma Mehboob. 22 (2) Weeks. May 26, 1978

Insaniyat. Screenplay & Directed by Shabab Kairanvi. Produced by: A. Hamid. Music: Manzoor-Ashraf. Lyrics: Khwaja Pervez, Nazim Panipati, Shabab Kairanvi. Story & Dialogue: Shatir Ghaznavi. Cast: Zeba, Waheed Murad, Tariq Aziz, Firdous, Raziya,Nannha, Asha, Tani, G. N. Butt, Salma Mumtaz, Hameed Vaeen, Sultan Rahi, Zeenat, Ali Ejaz (credited as Ali Baba). B&W. 30 (12) Weeks. February 20, 1967

Ishara. Directed, Produced & Written by Waheed Murad. Music: Sohail Rana. Lyrics & Dialogue: Masroor Anwar. Cast: Deeba, Waheed Murad, Rozina, Lehri, S. M. Saleem, Talat Hussain (debut), Neelofar, Zareen, Huma, Yasmeen, Sumbal, Shahin, Khurshid Kanwal, Naz Begum, Lashari, Hameed, Ansari, Hadi Imam. B&W (Partially colour). 33 (6). January 17, 1969

Ishq Mera Naa (Punjabi). Directed & Produced by M. Akram. Music: Nazir Ali. Script & Lyrics: Hazin Qadri. Cast: Waheed Murad, Aaliya, Iqbal Hassan, Ilyas Kashmiri, Naheed. 21 (3) Weeks (More than 75 in the Lahore Circuit). May 1, 1974

Izzat. Directed by Jafar Bukhari. Produced by Raheel Bari. Music: A. Hameed. Cast: Neelo, Waheed Murad, Talish, Sangeeta, Lehri, Tamanna, Qavi, Hanif, Kamal Irani, Ilyas Kashmiri, Masood Akhtar, Shahnawaz Senior. 23 (5) Weeks. January 10, 1975

Jaag Utha Insan. Directed by Sheikh Hassan. Produced by Habib-ur-Rahman. Music: Lal Muhammad-Iqbal. Lyrics, Screenplay & Dialogue: Dukhi Premnagri. Story: Makhdoom Husain. Cast: Muhammad Ali, Waheed

Murad, Zeba, Firdous, Ibrahim Nafis, Kamal Irani, Hassan Pahari, Chham Chham, . B&W. 36 (16) Weeks. May 20, 1966

Jaal. Directed by Iftikhar Khan. Produced by Waheed Murad. Music: Nazir Ali. Lyrics: Masroor Anwar, Khwaja Pervez. Written by Riaz Arshad. Cast: Nisho, Waheed Murad, Husna, S. M. Saleem, Saqi, Nannha, Shaista Qaisar, Rashid, Nazim, Aman Sufi, Changezi, Laddan. 39 (16). August 31, 1973

Jab Jab Phool Khiley. Directed by Iqbal Akhtar. Produced by Riaz Bukhari & Shariq Chaudhri. Music: M. Ashraf. Screenplay, Dialogue & Lyrics: Masroor Anwar. Written by Zahida Masroor. Cast: Muhammad Ali, Nadeem, Waheed Murad, Zeba, Mumtaz, Nayyar Sultana, Darpan, Kamal Irani, Ibrahim Nafis, Najma Mehboob, Shahnawaz, Nazli, Saqi, Khalid Saleem Mota, Jameel Bismil, Ejaz Akhter, Rehana Babri, Aliya Begum, Sultana Iqbal, Darakhshan, Nauran, Chakram. Child stars: Master Imran, Faisal Bokhari, Arshad, Tahir. 59 (10). November 21, 1975

Jahan Tum Wahan Hum. Directed & Produced by Pervez Malik. Music: Robin Ghosh. Lyrics: Masroor Anwar. Story & Dialogue: Danish Dervi. Cast: Shabnam, Waheed Murad, Nirala, Tamanna, S. M. Saleem, Latif Charlie, Naz Begum, Neelofar, Sumbul, Khurshid Kanwal, Hadi-ul-Islam, Badar, Saiqa, Azad, Agha Sarwar. B&W. 48 (13) Weeks. November 1, 1968

Jan-e-Arzoo. Directed by Qadeer Ghauri. Produced by G. A. Gul. Music: Master Inayat Hussain. Lyrics: Qateel Shifai. Written by Hasrat Lucknavi. Cast: Shamim Ara, Waheed Murad, Deeba, Santosh Kumar, Aslam Pervez, Salma Mumtaz, Lehri, Kamal Irani, Zumurrad, Akhtar Abbas, Tamanna, Nusrat Ara, Tahira, Chham Chham, . B&W. 18 (5). February 9, 1968

Jio Aur Jeene Do. Screenplay, Produced & Directed by Shamim Ara. Music: Robin Ghosh (Background score by M. Ilyas). Lyrics: Taslim Fazli. Story: Saba Fazli. Dialogue: Saba Fazli, Iqbal Rizvi, Khurshidullah, Masroor Anwar. Cast: Mumtaz, Ghulam Mohi-ud-din, Kaveeta, Waheed Murad, Shamim Ara, Nadeem, Munawar Saeed, Rangila, Lehri, Mustafa Qureshi, Zarqa, Firdausi, Shahnawaz, Khalid Salim Mota, Rashid, Badal. Child stars: Asif, Kamran, Baby Pomi, Naila. 21 (4). November 5, 1976

Joogi (Punjabi). Directed by Haider Chaudhry. Ismail. Produced by Chaudhry Ismail. Music: M. Ashraf. Lyrics: Khwaja Pervez. Written by Bashir Niaz. Cast: Waheed Murad, Aasiya, Bahar, Saiqa, Nannha, Ali Ejaz, Khayyam, Afzal Ahmad, Munawar Saeed, Ishrat Chaudhry, Saqi, Nasira, Neelofar, Nazo, Nazli, Hameed Chaudhry, Agha Dilraj, Gulraiz, Banka, Munir

Akhtar, Jabir. Child star: Nasir Butt. 18 (3) Weeks (More than 50 in the Lahore Circuit). April 25, 1975

Joshh. Directed by Iqbal Yusuf. Produced by Ghaffar Danawala & Iqbal Yusuf. Music: Mosleh-ud-Din. Lyrics: Kaleem Usmani. Written by Iqbal Rizvi. Cast: Sudhir, Zeba, Waheed Murad, Iqbal Yusuf, Hanif, Rukhsana, Rozina, Jaffry, Saqi, Santosh Russell, Adeeb, Kamal Irani, Latif Charlie, Faizy, Tarana, Nafeesa Noor, Khurshid. B&W. 25 (6) Weeks. April 2, 1966

Kala Dhanda Goray Loge.[1] Directed by Javed Sajjad. Produced by Kafait Hussain & Asif Khan. Music: Mehboob Pervez. Lyrics: Dr. Safi Hassan, Ph.D. Story: Kafait Hussain. Music: Mehboob Pervez. Cast: Muhammad Ali (uncredited voiceover in prologue), Asif Khan, Sangeeta, Waheed Murad, Patsy Stanley, Badar Munir, Maline Bloxham[2], Sameena (debuut), Zahid, Jaffery, Aman, Spencer Monty, Mike Paul[3], Suri Jackey, Gurjai Pal Singh, Kafait Hussain, Abbas Abid, Bashi Khan Hadi, Yaqoob, Nasim Asghar. Child stars: Joseph, Salman. 52 (8) Weeks. May 29, 1981

Kaneez. Directed by Hassan Tariq. Produced by Hassan Tariq & A. S. Afaqi. Music: Khalil Ahmad. Lyrics: Himayat Ali Shair & Agha Hashar Kashmiri (late). Written by A. S. Afaqi. Cast: Zeba, Waheed Murad, Muhammad Ali, Sabiha Khanum, Santosh Kumar, Talish, Amy, Lehri, Saqi, Adeeb, Aslam Pervez, Sabira Sultana, Faizy, Nasira, Nabila, Papoo, Master Billo, Gotam. B&W. 50 (16) Weeks. November 12, 1965

Khalish. Directed by Laeeq Akhtar. Produced by Sheikh Abdul Hafeez. Music: M. Ashraf. Lyrics: Kaleem Usmani. Story: Raziya Butt. Screenplay & Dialogue: B. H. Bukhari (assisted by Zahoor Zaidi). Cast: Waheed Murad, Rani, Sangeeta, Alauddin, Qavi, Waheeda Khan, Ragni, Ajmal, Atiya Sharaf, Rajni, Arslan, Jalil Afghani, Najma Mehboob, Meena Chaudhry, Surayya Soz. 56 (10) Weeks. January 27, 1972

Khamosh Nigahain. Directed by Jameel Akhtar. Produced by Sheikh Abd-ur-Rasheed. Music: M. Ashraf. Lyrics: Khwaja Pervez. Story, Dialogue & Screenplay: Saadat H. Zaidi. Cast: Waheed Murad, Rozina, Husna,

---

[1] A Pushto version of this movies was released separately: *Pakhtoon Pa Wilayat Kamba. Screenplay & Directed by Javed Sajjad. Produced by Asif Khan & Kafait Hussain*. Story: Dr. Safi Hassan, Ph.D. Cast: Asif Khan, Sangeeta, Waheed Murad, Patsy Stanley, Badar Munir, Melanie Bloxham, Sameena (debuut), Zahid, Jaffery, Aman, Spencer Monty, Mike Paul, Suri Jackey, Gurjai Pal Singh, Kafait Hussain, Abbas Abid, Bashi Khan Hadi, Yaqoob, Nasim Asghar, Liaquat Major. Child stars: Joseph, Salman. 8 (4) Weeks. October 23, 1981

[2] First name appears in the credits as 'Maline', which seems to be an error.

[3] Spelled as Meck Paul in credits, which seems to be an error.

Munawar Zarif, Zafar Masud Ali (debut), Abbas Nosha, Jaswant, Habiba, Aneela, Ashfaq. 16 (3) Weeks. June 4, 1971

Kharidar. Written & Directed by Jamshed Naqvi. Produced by Mahmood Jamshed. Music: M. Ashraf. Lyrics: Munir Niazi & Kaleem Usmani. Dialogue: Nasir Adeeb. Cast: Muhammad Ali, Waheed Murad, Deeba, Mumtaz, Habib, Nayyar Sultana, Aslam Pervez, Nannha, Kamal Irani, Seema, Azad, Asha Posley Zarqa, Khalid Salim Mota, Chakram, Kausar, Nishat, Suhail Bukhari, Pundit Shahid. Child star: Arshad Ali. 14 (3) Weeks. July 2, 1976

Khawab Aur Zindagi. Directed by Fareed Ahmed. Produced by Fasihuddin Kashmirwala. Music: A. Hameed. Lyrics: Qateel Shifai, Masroor Anwar. Story, Screenplay & Dialogue: Agha Hasan Imtisal. Cast: Shamim Ara, Waheed Murad, Masood Akhtar, Lehri, Saiqa, Atiya Sharaf, Sabiha Khanum, Aman Sufi. 21 (3) Weeks. June 8, 1973

Khuda Aur Mohabbat. Directed by Iqbal Yusuf. Produced by Malik Billoo & Iqbal Yusuf. Music: Tafoo. Story, Screenplay, Dialogue & Lyrics: Fayyaz Hashmi. Cast: Muhammad Ali, Babra Sharif, Waheed Murad, Ghulam Mohi-ud-din, Roohi Bano, Ghazal, Lehri, Tamanna, Najma Mehboob, Atiya Sharaf, Saqi, Inayat Anjum, Erum, Jahangir Mughal, Chakram, Mirza Shahi, Munna, Tari, Ashraf, Baba Azad, Pani Walker, Safdar. 41 (10) Weeks. October 20, 1978

Kiran Aur Kali. Directed by Zahid Shah. Produced by Ghazanfar Ali & Waseem Hassan. Music: Robin Ghosh (Background score: Karim Shahbuddin). Lyrics: Suroor Barabankvi, Taslim Fazli, Saeed Gilani. Story: Yaqoob Jamil. Screenplay & Dialogue: Masroor Anwar. Cast: Mohammad Ali, Shabnum, Waheed Murad, Lehri, Roohi Bano, Shaista Qaisar, Kamal Irani, Shahnawaz, Zeenat Yasmin, Arsh-e-Munir, Firdausi, Aftab, Rashid, Manzoor, Latif, Azra Babu, Mumtaz Kanwal, Anwar Beg, Cha Cha Notanki, Mushtaq Changezi, Adnan. Child star: Master Faraz. 58 (11) Weeks. September 4, 1981

Ladla. Directed by A. H. Siddiqui. Produced by Danish Dervi. Music: Lal Muhammad-Iqbal. Lyrics: Tanveer Naqvi, Sehba Akhtar, Kaif Rizvani, Masroor Anwar & Abdul Mannan (Bengali song). Screenplay, Story & Dialogue: Danish Dervi. Cast: Waheed Murad, Shabnam, Santosh, Sabiha Khanum Talish, Lehri, Nirala, Tamanna, Talat Siddiqi, Azad, Neelofar, Khurshid Kanwal. B&W. 38 (10). June 13, 1969

Laila Majnu. Directed by Hassan Tariq. Produced by Syed Ata Ullah Shah Hashmi. Music: Nisar Bazmi. Script & Lyrics: Saifuddin Saif. Cast: Rani, Waheed Murad, Shahid, Masood Akhtar, Talish, Alla-ud-Din, Zammurad, Nannha, Nasira, Rashid, Jalil Afghani, Mizla, Ishrat Chaudhry. 19 (3) Weeks. October 18, 1974.

Maa Baap. Directed by Khaleel Kaiser. Produced by S. Ata Ullah Shah Hashmi. Music: Tasaddaq. Lyrics: Qateel Shifai. Story & Screenplay: Qamar Ajnalvi. Dialogue: Riaz Shahid & Qamar Ajnalvi. Cast: Zeba, Waheed Murad, Talat Siddiqui, Yousaf Khan, Zumurrad, Alla-ud-Din, Rangila, Jugnu. B&W. 33 (11) Weeks. September 22, 1967

Maa Beta. Screenplay & Directed by Hassan Tariq. Produced by Nooruddin Kisat, Hassan Tariq & Waheed Murad. Music: Sohail Rana. Lyrics: Masroor Anwar. Story & Dialogue: Agha Hasan Imtisal. Cast: Sabiha Khanum Waheed Murad, Santosh Kumar, Rani, Masood Akhtar, Meena, Rangila, Saiqa, Gotum, Murad, Tipoo, Santosh, Lehri. B&W. 19 (4) Weeks. September 26, 1969

Maang Meri Bhar Do. Screenplay & Directed by Gouhar Ali. Produced by Muzaffar Husain. Music: Amir Sultan Wazir. Lyrics: Mauj Lakhnavi. Story: Khurshidullah. Dialogue: Amin Mirza. Cast: Muhammad Ali, Shabnam, Waheed Murad, Ishrat Chaudhry, Lehri, Naz Begum, Adnan, S. Mughal, Adeel (debut), Tehmina (debut), Shahanshah (debut), Arfi (debut), Fareed Qureshi (debut), Ali Imran (debut), Peeno (debut), Anjum Shad (debut), Sadaf (debut), Shamsi (debut), Taj Rana (debut). Child stars: Arshad Hussain, Shaheen, Shazia, Faisal, Ayaz Tirmizi, Akhtar Shah, Nawab Ali, Saleem, Saithiya, Asif. 25 (1) Weeks. May 27, 1983

Mamta. Direction, screenplay and story: Saqlain Razvi. Produced by Sibtain Rizvi. Cast: Habib, Naghma, Yasmin, Waheed Murad, Master Jimmy, Ajmal, Rangila, Asad Bukhari, Saqi, Laddan, Jafri, Ami Minwala, Sultan Rahi, Tangoo. B&W. 13 (4) Weeks. March 4, 1964

Mastana Mahi (Punjabi). Directed by Iftikhar Khan. Produced by Waheed Murad. Music: Nazeer Ali. Script & Lyrics: Hazin Qadri. Cast: Waheed Murad, Naghma, Aaliya, Munawar Zarif, Asad Bukhari, Taya Barkat, Rangoon Wallah, Muhammad Yusuf (credited as Yusuf Qasim), Ajmal, Razziya, Khalifa Nazeer, Rasheed Zarif, Asha, Chauhan. B&W. 10/40 Weeks (More than 50 in the Lahore Circuit). September 24, 1971

Mastani Mahbooba. Directed by Laeeq Akhtar. Produced by Azra Jabeen. Music: Nisar Bazmi. Lyrics: Masroor Anwar. Cast: Sangeeta, Waheed

Murad, Munawar Zarif, Kaveeta, Aslam Pervez, Waheeda Khan, Saqi, Sabira, Shakir, Shahnawaz, Haroon Pasha, Nishi, Aman Sufi. 21 (3) Weeks. August 16, 1974

Mehboob Mera Mastana. Directed by Saqlain Razvi. Produced by Tariq Ifzal. Music: Nashad. Lyrics: Taslim Fazli, Riaz-ur-Rehman Saghar. Written by Agha Hasan Imtisal. Cast: Aasiya, Waheed Murad, Sangeeta, Deeba, Lehri, Talish, Masood Akhtar, Nannha, Ali Ejaz, Asifa, Andleeb, Waheeda Khan, Atiya Sharaf, Meena Dawood, Musarrat Shaheen, Albela, Nagina Khanum, Naveed, Najma Roomani, Zeshan, Azam, Fareeda, Rubeena, Sabu, Banka, Anwar Majeed. 15 (1) Weeks. May 28, 1976

Mere Apney. Produced & Directed by Shamim Ara. Music: Nisar Bazmi. Lyrics: Shevan Razvi, Masroor Anwar, Taslim Fazli. Cast: Shamim Ara, Shahid, Mumtaz, Waheed Murad, Asif Raza Mir, Talish, Tamanna, Qavi, Saqi. 27 (3) Weeks. May 8, 1981

Mohabbat Zindgi Hai. Directed by Iqbal Akhtar. Produced by Begum Riaz Bukhari. Music: M. Ashraf. Screenplay, Dialogue & Lyrics: Masroor Anwar. Story: Zahida Masroor. Cast: Zeba, Muhammad Ali, Mumtaz, Waheed Murad, Nayyar Sultana, Qavi, Lehri, Zeenat, Kamal Irani, Aadil, Saqi, Shahnawaz, Zarqa, Khalid Salim Mota, Chakram, Mizla, Shazia, Tabassum, Naureen, Naina, Chabila, Imdad Husain, K. Kumar. 59 (12) Weeks. June 6, 1975

Mulaqat. Directed by Laeeq Akhtar. Produced by Sheikh Abdul Hafeez. Music: Nisar Bazmi. Lyrics: Kaleem Usmani. Written by Zakir Husain. Cast: Waheed Murad, Nisho, Qavi, Lehri, Munawar Saeed, Afzal Ahmad, Atiya Sharaf, Najma Mehboob, Meena Chaudhry, Aman Sufi, Khalid Saleem Mota, Hassan Raza Khan, Ijaz Malik, Mahmood Jafry, Naheed Ahmad, Baby Huma. 23 (6) Weeks. April 20, 1973

Naag Aur Nagin. Screenplay & Directed by Hassan Tariq. Produced by Begum Rattan Kumar. Music: Nisar Bazmi. Lyrics: Saifuddin Saif. Story & Dialogue: Aziz Meeruthi. Cast: Rani, Waheed Murad, Nayyar Sultana, Alla-ud-din, Kaveeta, Aslam Pervez, Shahid, Zeenat, Ilyas Kashmiri, Mezla, Parveen Boby, Imdad, Hamid, Goutam, Ladla, Abushan, Abid Shah. Child stars: Ali Imran, Shahid, Kuki. 18 (4) Weeks. March 26, 1976

Naag Muni. Directed by Raza Mir. Produced by Afzal Hussain & Raza Mir. Music: Nisar Bazmi. Lyrics: Habib Jalib, Fayyaz Hashmi, Masroor Anwar. Story based on Waheeda Naseem's novel of the same title. Screenplau Najam-ul-Hasan. Dialogue: Ahmad Rahi & Masroor Anwar. Cast: Waheed

Murad, Rani, Rukhsana, Sangeeta, Talish, Qavi, Masud Akhtar, Najam-ul-Hasan, Jalil Afghani, Arslan, Saqi, Naina, Baby Najmi, Zahid Sheikh. 23 (6) Weeks. April 7, 1972

Nannah Farishta. Directed by K. Khursheed & M. A. Ali. Produced by Nooruddin Kisat & K. Khurshid. Music: M. Ashraf. Lyrics: Kaleem Usmani. Story: Jalil Afghani. Screenplay & Dialogue: Bashir Niaz. Cast: Muhammad Ali, Deeba, Waheed Murad, Nayyar Sultana, Munawar Zarif, Nimmo, Qavi, Ali Ejaz, Atiya Sharaf, Hanif, Imran Adil, Jalil Afghani, Zaigham, Iqbal Durrani, Chakram, Pani Walker, Rashid, Mehboob, Saqib, Agha Shahi, Nazli. Child stars: Tasawar Mir, Suhail Abbas. 28 (4) Weeks. October 18, 1974

Naseeb Apna Apna. Directed by Qamar Zaidi. Produced by Waheed Murad. Music: Lal Muhammad-Iqbal. Lyrics: Masroor Anwar. Written by Iqbal Rizvi. Cast: Shabnam, Waheed Murad, Zamarrud, Saqi, Nirala, S. M. Saleem, Tamanna, Muhammad Yusuf (credited as Yusuf Qasim), Rangila, Nihal, Zoni, Aneela, Ansari, Shaheen, Zarin. B&W. 32 (11) Weeks. April 3, 1970

Nazrana. Directed by Nazar Shabab. Produced by A. Hamid. Music: M. Ashraf. Lyrics: Qateel Shifai. Story & Screenplay: Shabab Kairanvi (based on the short story 'Fashion' by Ahmad Nadeem Qasmi). Cast: Rani, Ghulam Mohi-ud-din, Waheed Murad, Neelo, Nayyar Sultan, Nannha, Bindya, Tamanna, Seema, Masood Akhtar, Hanif, Meena Dawood, Roomana, Ali Ejaz, Chakram, Agha Dilraj, Azhar Zaidi, Majeed Shah. 33 (7) Weeks. June 9, 1978

Neend Hamari Khwab Tumhare. Directed & Produced by K. Khurshid (Executive Producer: Sh. Tassaduq Hussain. Music: M. Ashraf. Lyrics: Kaleem Usmani. Written by Bashir Niaz based on basic idea from Mistry Ghulam Muhammad. Cast: Deeba, Waheed Murad, Aaliya, Nirala, Qavi, Talish, Latif Charlie, Zeenat, Shahida, A. Shah, Bachu Bhai, Pani Walker, M. D. Sheikh, Iltaf, Javed Butt, Fazal Haq. 51 (15) Weeks. January 1, 1971

Nishani. Directed by Jamshed Naqvi. Produced by: Muhammad Jamil. Music: Juzi Anjum. Lyrics: Taslim Fazli. Story & Screenplay: Zafar Nadeem. Dialogue: Rasheed Sajid. Cast: Shabnam, Waheed Murad, Nayyar Sultana, Aslam Pervez, Qavi, Tariq Aziz, Irfan Khoosat, Meena Shori, Roomana, Chakram, Tabassum, Anwar Ali, Saadia, Ejaz Akhtar, Naina, Naini, Saiqa, Albela, Khalid Salim Mota, Sanam, Shagufta, Aman, Kiran, Kausar, Ladla. 26 (3) Weeks. April 6, 1979

Parakh. Directed by Jan Muhammad. Produced by S. M. Hussain. Music: Kamal Ahmad. Lyrics: Taslim Fazli. Story: Jalil Afghani. Screenplay & Dialogue: Bashir Niaz. Cast: Rani, Waheed Murad, Asif Khan, Usman Pirzada, Naveen Tajik, Tammana, Saqi, Nannha, Dildar Pervaiz Bhatti, Qavi, Roomana, Jalil Afghani, Rashid, Veena, Najma Parveen, Yahya, Nazir Irani. 52 (8) Weeks. April 7, 1978

Parastish. Directed by Aziz-ul-Hassan. Produced by Nasim Ahmed. Music: Wajid Ali Nashad. Lyrics: Taslim Fazli. Story: Haroon Pasha. Screenplay & Dialogue: Saleem Shahzad. Cast: Nadeem, Mumtaz, Waheed Murad, Deeba, Nayyar Sultana, Munawar Saeed, Nannha, Khalid Salim Mota, Saqi, Bobby Maqbool. 21 (2) Weeks. January 14, 1977

Parwah Nein. Directed by Iftikhar Khan. Produced by Zulfiqar Ali Khan, Zia Qamar & Rashid Khan. Music: Nazir Ali. Lyrics: Hazin Qadri, Khwaja Pervez, Written by Nasir Adeeb. Cast: Yusuf Khan, Mustafa Qureshi, Waheed Murad, Mumtaz, Kaveeta, Sabiha Khanum, Talish, Ilyas Kashmiri, Ali Ejaz, Saqi, Asad, Nasurllah Butt, Mustafa Tind, Haidar Abbas. Child stars: Badal Shah, Nadeem Mohsin, Mahmood. 15 (3) Weeks. June 12, 1981

Phir Chand Nikley Ga. Directed by Rafiq Razvi. Produced by Mehmood-ul-Haq. Music: Sohail Rana. Lyrics: Anjum Keranvi. Story: Mubin-ul-Haq Siddiqi. Dialogue: Iqbal Rizvi. Screenplay: Saleem Ahmad. Cast: Deeba, Waheed Murad, Rozina, Nirala, Hanif, Shah Nawaz, Azad, Tamanna, Ibrahim Nafis, Mehmood Ali B&W. 21 (4) Weeks. October 9, 1970.

Phir Subah Hogi. Directed by Rafiq Razvi. Produced by: Rafiq Chaudhry. Music: Nashad. Lyrics: Fayyaz Hashmi, Masroor Anwar, Shahid Dehlavi, Sehba Akhtar. Story, Screenplay & Dialogue: Agha Nazir Kavish. Cast: Deeba, Waheed Murad, Iqbal Yusuf, Ibrahim Nafis, Talat Siddiqui, Nirala, Kamal Irani, Rashid, Samia Naz, Naz Begum, Shakila, Chham Chham. B&W. 41 (11) Weeks. August 9, 1967

Phool Mere Gulshan Ka. Directed by Iqbal Akhtar. Produced by Begum Riaz Bukhari, G. K. Afridi, Mian Fayyaz. Music: M. Ashraf. Story: Zahida Masroor. Screenplay, Dialogue & Lyrics: Masroor Anwar. Cast: Zeba, Muhammad Ali, Waheed Murad, Nisho, Nadeem, Saira (debut), Aurangzeb, Lehri, Tamanna, Kamal Irani, Master Khalid. 62 (18) Weeks. July 12, 1974

Piyari. Directed by Jamshed Naqvi. Produced by Azra Chaudhary. Music: M. Ashraf. Lyrics: Taslim Fazli, Khwaja Pervez. Written by Syed Noor. Cast: Shabnam, Waheed Murad, Ghulam Mohi-ud-din, Nisho, Naghma, Hanif, Qavi, Seema, Saqi, Jameel Fakhri, Humayun Qureshi, Khalid Salim Mota,

Ejaz Akhtar, Sanam, Chun Chun, Musarrat Jabeen. Child star: Baby Chanda. 61 (8) Weeks. December 12, 1980

Pyar Hi Pyar. Written & Directed by Rafiq Ali Rakhan. Produced by Aasiya Ikram. Music: Nisar Bazmi. Lyrics: Taslim Fazli. Dialogue: Riaz Arshad. Cast: Aasiya, Waheed Murad, Shazia (debut), Alla-ud-din, Adeeb, Munawar Saeed, Khalifa Nazeer, Meena Dawood, Tani, Mustafa, Seema, Farida, Nishi. 51 (15) Weeks. February 8, 1974

Raja Ki Ayai Gi Barat. Directed by Iftikhar Khan. Produced by S. M. Ashfaq. Music: M. Ashraf. Lyrics: Taslim Fazli. Written by Syed Noor. Cast: Mumtaz, Waheed Murad, Muhammad Ali, Sabiha Khanum, Qavi, Adeeb, Chakram, Khalid Salim Mota, Suman Dar Khan, Abu Shah, Iqbal, Anwar Majid, Samina, Tari, . 18 (2) Weeks. April 27, 1979

Rastey Ka Pather. Directed by M. A. Rasheed. Associate Director & Producer: Ejaz Rasheed. Music: Nashad. Dialogue & Lyrics: Masroor Anwar. Story: Shahbaz Bakhat. Cast: Nisho, Waheed Murad, Sultan Rahi, Sabiha Khanum, Roohi Bano, Aslam Pervez, Qavi, Lehri, Rangila, Masood Akhtar, Ishrat Chaudhry, Tamanna, Ibrahim Nafis, Saqi, Asif Khan, Shahnawaz, Nazli, Zarqa, Amber, Salim, Jaggi. 23 (3) Weeks. March 5, 1976

Rim Jhim. Directed by Qamar Zaidi. Produced by Khursheed Sajjad. Music: Nashad. Lyrics: Shevan Rizvi & Qateel Shifai. Story, Screenplay & Dialogue: Riaz Farshori. Cast: Waheed Murad, Rozina, Zamarrud, Qazi Wajid, Meena Chaudhry, Samia Naz, Nini, Naz Begum, Santosh Russell, Zahoor Ahmad, Naisr Khan, Mahmood Ali, Kamal Irani, Azad. B&W. 14 (4). January 22, 1971

Rishta Hai Pyar Ka. Directed by Qamar Zaidi. Produced by Iqbal Butt. Music: Nashad. Lyrics: Fayyaz Hashmi. Story: Saleem Ahmad. Cast: Zeba, Waheed Murad, Trannum, Kamal Irani, Iqbal Yusuf, Farida, Hanif, Adeeb, Nehal, Sentosh Russell, Shida Imam, Girj Babu. B&W. 29 (6) Weeks. October 6, 1967

Saaz-o-Awaz. Directed by M. Hashim. Produced by Muhammad Ali (not to be confused with the actor). Music: Hassan Latif. Lyrics: Habib Jalib, Akbar Banglori. Cast: Rani, Waheed Murad, Habib, Talish. B&W. 13 (4) Weeks. April 30, 1965

Saheli. Lyrics, Written, Produced & Directed by Shabab Kairanvi. Music: M. Ashraf. Dialogue: Riaz-ur-Rehman Saghar. Cast: Shabnam, Waheed Murad, Rani, Ghulam Mohi-ud-din, Nannha, Shehla Gil, Hanif, Aurangzeb Laghari, M. D. Sheikh, Tamanna, Ibrahim Nafis, Waheeda Khan, Ilyas Najam,

Anwar Ali, Pervaiz Tariq, Maqbool, Majeed Shah, Sadiq Ali. 56 (16) Weeks. February 17, 1978

Sajjan Kamla (Punjabi). Directed by M. Akram. Produced by Farooq Mian & Mushtaq Mirza. Music: Nazir Ali. Script & Lyrics: Hazin Qadri. Cast: Aaliya, Waheed Murad, Munawar Zarif, Talish, Hanif, Munawar Saeed, Afzaal Ahmad, Atiya Sharaf, Ishrat Chaudhry, Shahnawaz, Saba, Khalifa Nazeer, Surayya Khan, Taya Barkat, Sajan, Gulrez, Nazo, Zarqa, Munir Zarif, Khalid Abbas Dar, Shehzad, Iqbal Bukhari, Farhi (debut), Chandpuri, Surayya Khan. 14 (2) Weeks. December 12, 1975

Salgirah. Directed by Qamar Zaidi. Produced by Begum Najma Hasan & Qamar Zaidi. Music: Nashad. Lyrics: Shawan Rizvi & Taslim Fazli[1]. Screenplay: Saleem Ahmad. Story: Shams Hanfi. Dialogue: Shams Hanfi & Iqbal Rizvi. Cast: Shamim Ara, Waheed Murad, Tariq Aziz, Nirala, Nighat Sultana, Kamal Irani, S. M. Saleem, Agha Jan, Latif Charlie, Naz Begum, Rahila, Chhum Chhum, Hashmi, Farida Anjum, Rehana Siddiqi, Nihal. 61 (20). February 14, 1969

Samandar. Directed by Rafiq Razvi. Produced by Waheed Murad. Music: Deebu. Lyrics: Sehba Akhtar. Story: Agha Nazir Kawish. Cast: Shabnam, Waheed Murad, Hanif, Rozina, Rashid, S. M. Saleem, Nirala, Qurban Jilani, Aftab, Rahila, Naz Begum, Agha Sarwar, Hamid, Hasan Pahari, Ansari . B&W. 37 (9) Weeks. March 10, 1968

Sayyoni Mera Mahi (Punjabi). Directed by Iftikhar Khan. Produced by Irfan Hamid Butt. Music: Nazir Ali. Lyrics: Hazin Qadri. Cast: Aaliya, Waheed Murad, Munawar Zarif, Sabiha Khanum, Alla-ud-din, Rukhsana, Nayyar Sultana, Seema, Tani, Qavi, Rangila. 12 (2) Weeks. May 31, 1974

Shabana. Directed by Nazar Shabab. Produced by A. Hamid. Music: M. Ashraf. Lyrics: Taslim Fazli. Story & Screenplay: Shabab Kairanvi. Dialogue: Riaz-ur-Rehman Saghar. Cast: Babra Sharif, Waheed Murad, Shahid, Nannha, Masood Akhtar, Ishrat Chaudhry, Kamal Irani, Nazim, Riaz-ur-Rehman Saghar, Zarqa, Parveen Boby, Seema, Tamanna, Chakram, Tango. 101 (38) Weeks. November 12, 1976

Shama. Directed by Nazar Shabab. Produced by A. Hamid. Music: M. Ashraf. Lyrics: Taslim Fazli. Story & Screenplay: Shabab Kairanvi. Dialogue: Riaz-ur-Rehman Saghar. Cast: Muhammad Ali, Nadeem, Waheed Murad,

[1] It is written 'Tasneem Fazli' in the credits, apparently by mistake.

Deeba, Babra Sharif, Zeba, Alla-ud-din, Tamanna, Neelofar, Chakram, Saqi, Khalid Salim Mota, Farzana. 65 (18) Weeks. December 25, 1974

Sheeshey Ka Ghar. Directed by Nazrul Islam. Produced by Muhammad Ajmal Choudhry & Muhammad Aslam Butt. Music: Master Abdullah. Lyrics: Qateel Shifai & Taslim Fazli. Written by Agha Hasan Imtisal. Cast: Mumtaz, Shahid, Waheed Murad, Nannha, Rozina, Ishrat Chaudhry, Hanif, Afzal Ahmad, Chakori, Shahnawaz. 23 (3) Weeks. June 2, 1978

Soorat Aur Seerat. Directed by Iqbal Yusuf. Produced by Muzaffar Hussain, Mushtaq Ahmed, Muhammad Nazir. Music: M. Ashraf. Lyrics: Taslim Fazli. Written by Khurshidullah. Cast: Sudhir, Muhammad Ali, Waheed Murad, Mumtaz, Nayyar Sultana, Nisho, Lehri, Ilyas Kashmiri, Mustafa Qureshi, Hanif, Meena Dawood, Jalil Afghani, Fakhra, Sikander, Nauroze, Faizy, S. Gul, Raj Multani, Nasir Khan, Agha Sajjad, Anila Nafees, Aziz Yusuf, Malta, Rashik Ali, Mangole, Zilfiqar Ali, Gul Khan. Child stars: Asif, Adnan. 50 (6) Weeks. October 7, 1975

Surrayya Bhopali. Screenplay & Directed by Hassan Tariq. Produced by Hassan Shah. Music: A. Hameed. Lyrics: Saifuddin Saif. Story & Dialogue: Agha Hasan Imtisal. Cast: Waheed Murad, Shahid, Rani, Husna, Alla-ud-din, Talish, Aslam Pervez, Bahar, Ishrat Chaudhry, Nirala, Saqi, Meena Dawood, Laddan, Pani Walker. 20 (4) Weeks. July 16, 1976

Tarana. Produced & Directed by Zafar Shabab. Produced by Music: M. Ashraf. Lyrics: Saeed Gilani, Riaz-ur-Rehman Saghar, Masroor Anwar. Story & Screenplay: Shabab Kairanvi. Dialogue: Riaz-ur-Rehman Saghar. Cast: Rani, Waheed Murad, Amjad (debut), Ghulam Mohi-ud-din, Nannha, Tamanna, Bahar. Seema, Meena Shori, Ibrahim Nafis, Tani, Zill-e-Subhan, Najma Roomani, Rukhsana Multani, Shahnawaz, Samar, 46 (8) Weeks. March 9, 1979

Tum Salamat Raho. Directed by M. A. Rasheed. Produced by Ejaz Rasheed. Music: Nashad. Dialogue & Lyrics: Masroor Anwar. Story: Younus Rahi. Cast: Muhammad Ali, Waheed Murad, Aasiya, Mumtaz, Nayyar Sultana, Rehman, Adeeb, Saqi, Lehri, Nannha, Nirala, Tamanna, Zarqa, Chhabela, Ejaz Rasheed, Zafri, Rehana, Fauzia. 51 (15) Weeks. May 10, 1974

Tumhi Ho Mehboob Mere. Directed by Shabab Kairanvi. Music: M. Ashraf. Lyrics: Khwaja Pervez, Ehsan Danish. Cast: Deeba, Waheed Murad, Rozina, Qavi, Rashid Umar, M. D. Sheikh, Khurshid Shaukat, Waheeda, Meena. 17 (5) Weeks. February 23, 1969

Usay Dekha Usay Chaha. Directed by Pervez Malik. Produced by Aslam Saeed. Music: Sohail Rana. Lyrics: Fayyaz Hashmi, Masroor Anwar. Written by Masroor Anwar. Cast: Rozina, Waheed Murad, Nirala, Lehri, Tamanna, Zakia Khanum, Santosh Russell, Andleeb, Niggo. 16 (2) Weeks. September 6, 1974

Waade Ki Zanjeer. Produced & Directed by Shabab Kairanvi. Music: M. Ashraf. Lyrics: Qateel Shifai, Masroor Anwar. Short Story: Sattar Tahir. Dialogue: Riaz-ur-Rehman Saghar. Adaptation for film & Screenplay: Shabab Kairanvi. Cast: Muhammad Ali, Anjuman (debut), Waheed Murad, Sabiha Khanum, Masood Akhtar, Tamanna, Nannha, Ali Ejaz, Shehla Gil, Zill-e-Subhan, Ibrahim Nafis, Bindya, Ghayur Akhtar, Samar, Chakram, Munna, Majeed Shah, Khumar, Shamsi Malik, Bushra Bukhari. Child stars: Master Jawwad, Talat. 33 (5) Weeks. February 4, 1979

Wahda. Directed by Aslam Dar. Produced by Nasim Asghar Jaura. Music: Kamal Ahmad. Lyrics: Taslim Fazli, Fayyaz Hashmi, Riaz-ur-Rehman Saghar. Story: Agha Hasan Imtisal. Dialogue: Aziz Meeruthi. Cast: Waheed Murad, Aasiya, Deeba, Lehri, Munawar Zarif, Alla-ud-din, Saiqa, Atiya Sharaf, Saqi, Meena Shori, Asifa, Albela, Munir Zarif, Mansoor, Zahid Khan, Neelum, Neelum Akhtar, Talat, Hamid Husain, Tango, Bashir (Mota). 34 (5) Weeks. June 4, 1976

Waqt. Produced & Directed by Zafar Shabab. Music: Nashad. Lyrics: Taslim Fazli. Story & Screenplay: Shabab Kairanvi. Dialogue: Riaz-ur-Rehman Saghar. Cast: Babra Sharif, Waheed Murad, Kaveeta, Shamim Ara, Habib, Nannha, Tariq (debut), Najma, Rehan, Hanif, Jamil Fakhri, Najma Mehboob, Tamanna, Shahnawaz, Parveen Boby, Badee-uz-Zaman, Chakram, Pundit Shahid, Naina, Sadiq Ali Shah, Chilly, Zahida. Child stars: Kamran Abbasi, Asif. 35 (7) Weeks. April 30, 1976

Wohti Jee (Punjabi). Produced & Directed by M. J. Rana. Music: Bakhshi Wazir. Lyrics: Hazin Qadri, Sahil. Story: Sheikh Iqbal. Dialogue: Hasnain Hashmi. Cast: Waheed Murad, Mumtaz, Ali Ejaz, Musarrat Shaheen, Sabiha Khanum, Asha Poslay, Alla-ud-Din, Munawar Saeed, Ilyas Kashmiri, Majeed Zarif, Nazli, Ladla, Sheikh Iqbal, Ladla, Banka, Munna. Child stars: Master Khurram, Aneela. 13 (1) Weeks. May 14, 1982

Yahan Se Wahan Tak. Produced & Directed by Syed Kamal. Music: Wajahat Attre. Lyrics: Masroor Anwar. Written by Hasina Moin. Additional dialogue: Iqbal Rizvi. Cast: Mumtaz, Kamal, Waheed Murad, Asif Khan,

Ali Ejaz, Nadira, Asifa, Chakram, Shakil, Aman Sufi, Teresa, Zainy. 30 (3) Weeks. February 25, 1979

Zaib-un-Nisa. Directed by Fareed Ahmed. Produced by Muhammad Akram Choudhry. Music: Master Inayat Husain. Lyrics: Kaleem Usmani. Written by Naqi Mustafa. Cast: Waheed Murad, Shamim Ara, Aaliya, Saleem Nasir, Munawar Saeed, Sheikh Iqbal, Munir Zarif, Talish, Tamanna, Fazil Butt, Iqbal Durrani, Jalil Afghani, Shah Nawaz, Jamil Bismil, Irfan Khoost, Ghayyur Akhtar, Abbu Shah. 18 (2). July 2, 1976

Zalzala. Directed by Iqbal Yusuf. Produced by M. Riaz Akhtar. Music: Tafoo. Lyrics: Khwaja Pervez. Story: Bashir Jaffery. Screenplay: Khurshidullah. Dialogue: Rashid Sajid. Cast: Sudhir, Sultan Rahi, Waheed Murad, Asif Khan, Rani, Seema, Hanif, Kamal Irani, Ilyas Kashmiri, Adeeb, Musarrat Shaheen, Ishrat Chaudhry, Surrayya Khan, Humayun Qureshi, Zahir Shah, Wasi Khan, Khalid Butt, Dimple, Akhtar. Child star: Master Adnan. 24 (4) Weeks. March 13, 1987

Zamir. Directed by Iqbal Akhtar. Produced by S. M. Hasan & Mehboob Ali. Music: Nashad. Lyrics: Taslim Fazli, Saba Fazli. Screenplay & Dialogue: Saba Fazli. Cast: Muhammad Ali, Waheed Murad, Roohi Bano, Deeba, Ghazal, Tamanna, Lehri. March 7, 1980

Zindagi Aik Safar Hai. Screenpplay & Direction by S. M. Yusuf. Produced by Latif Butt. Music: A. Hameed. Lyrics: Qateel Shifaim, Riaz-ur-Rehman Saghar. Story by Sikandar Hayat. Dialogue: Maqbool Jalees, Khusheed Ullah. Cast: Shamim Ara, Waheed Murad, Deeba, Ejaz, Iqbal Yusuf, Azad, Muhammad Yusuf, Arsh-e-Munir, Fyzee, Agha Jan, Sikander, S. Gul. 34 (12) Weeks. September 1, 1972

Zubeda. Directed & Produced by Aslam Dar. Music: Kamal Ahmad. Lyrics: Riaz-ur-Rehman Saghar, Qateel Shifai, Fayyaz Hashmi. Story & Dialogue: Aziz Meeruthi. Cast: Nisho, Waheed Murad, Babra Sharif, Sabiha Khanum, Lehri, Rangila, Aslam Pervez, Meena Shori, Saqi, Musarrat Shaheen, Shahida, Nazneen, Imran Rahi, Khalid Butt. Child stars: Baby Rafiq, Shams Zaidi. 25 (5) Weeks. January 16, 1975

Chronological

1962
Aulad, August 10
1963
Daaman, May 13
1964
Mamta, March 4
Heera Aur Pather, December 11

1965
Bahu Begum, March 2
Doctor, March 12
Saaz-o-Awaz, April 30
Eid Mubarak, July 2
Kaneez, November 12

1966
Armaan, March 18,
Honhaar, March 25
Joshh, April 2
Jaag Utha Insan, May 20
Bhaiya, October 14

1967
Insaniyat, February 20
Dewar Bhabhi, May 5
Ehsaan, June 30
Doraha, August 25
Phir Subha Hogi, August 9
Maan Baap, September 22
Rishta Hai Pyar Ka, October 6

1968
Jan-e-Arzoo, February 9
Samandar, March 10
Dil Mera Dharkan Teri, April 26
Jahan Tum Wahan Hum,
    November 1

1969
Ishara, January 17

Salgirah, February 14
Tumhi Ho Mehboob Mere,
    February 23
Ladla, June 13
Andaleeb, August 29
Ik Nagina, September 9
Maan Beta, September 26

1970
Afsana, February 6
Be Wafa, March 20
Naseeb Apna Apna, April 3
Anjuman, July 31
Phir Chand Nikley Ga, October 9
Chand Suraj, December 25

1971
Neend Hamari Khwab Tumhare,
    January 1
Rim Jhim, January 22
Afshan, March 12
Khamosh Nigahain, June 4
Mastana Mahi (Punjabi),
    September 24

1972
Khalish, January 27
Hill Station, March 10
Naag Muni, April 7
Daulat Aur Duniya, April 28
Bandagi, June 23
Baharo Phool Barsao, August 11
Zindagi Aik Safar Hai, September
    1

1973
Mulaqat, April 20
Khawab Aur Zindagi, June 8
Jaal, August 31
Anhoni, December 21

1974
Pyar Hi Pyar, February 8
Ishq Mera Naa, May 1
Tum Salamat Raho, May 10
Sayyoni Mera Mahi (Punjabi),
   May 31
Phool Mere Gulshan Ka, July 12
Mastani Mahbooba, August 16
Usay Dekha Usay Chaha,
   September 6
Nannah Farishta, October 18
Laila Majnu, October 18
Haqeeqat, November 1
Dushman, November 8
Deedar, November 15
Shama, December 25

1975
Izzat, January 10
Joogi (Punjabi), April 25
Mohabbat Zindgi Hai, June 6
Soorat Aur Seerat, October 7
Dil Ruba, October 7
Jab Jab Phool Khiley, November
   21
Sajjan Kamla (Punjabi),
   December 12
Zubeda, January 16

1976
Rastey Ka Pather, March 5
Naag Aur Nagin, March 26
Mehboob Mera Mastana, May 28
Waqt, April 30
Wahda, June 4
Zaib-un-Nisa, July 2
Kharidar, July 2
Surrayya Bhopali, July 16
Akh Lari Bado Badi (Punjabi),
   September 26
Jio Aur Jeene Do, November 5
Shabana, November 12

Goonj Uthi Shehnai, November
   19
Aap Ka Khadim, March 12

1977
Parastish, January 14
Apney Huay Paraey, December 2

1978
Aadmi, February 10
Saheli, February 17
Parakh, April 7
Insaan Aur Shaitan, May 26
Sheeshay Ka Ghar, June 2
Nazrana, June 9
Khuda Aur Mohabbat, October 20
Awaaz, October 27

1979
Bahen Bhai, January 19
Waade Ki Zanjeer, February 4
Yahan Se Wahan Tak, February
   25
Tarana, March 9
Nishani, April 6
Raja Ki Ayai Gi Barat, April 27
Aurat Raj, July 13

1980
Zamir, March 7
Chotee Nawab, March 14
Bandhan, March 21
Badnaam, October 3
Piyari, December 12

1981
Anokha Daaj (Punjabi), February
   27
Mere Apney, May 8
Gunman, May 8
Dil Ney Phir Yaad Kiya, May 15
Kala Dhanda Goray Loge, May
   29
Parvah Nein, June 12
Kiran Aur Kali, September 4

Ghairao, October 9

Pakhtoon Pa Wilayat Kamba,
    October 23

1982

I Love You, March 12

Aahat, April 16

Wohti Jee (Punjabi), May 14

1983

Maang Meri Bhar Do, May 27

1985

Hero, January 11

1987

Zalzala, March 13

References

Textual

[Anonymous]. 'In Memoriam: Adieu to a veteran and a patriot.' *Dawn,* February 15, 2009. Retrieved on May 7, 2015 http://www.dawn.com/news/860651/in-memoriam-adieu-to-a-veteran-and-a-patriot

Ahmad, Absar. 'Ahmad Rushdi – Pakistani qaumi naghmat ka awalleen badshah' (Urdu). *Nigar Weekly,* Karachi, April 19, 2015

Ahmad, Deputy Nazeer (Urdu). *Mirat-ul Uroos* [Bride's Mirror]. *N.D.* Soft copy retrieved on May 9, 2015 from https://archive.org/details/MiratUlUroos

Ahmed, Akbar S. *Jinnah, Pakistan and Islamic Identity: The search for Saladin.* 1997. London: Routledge, 2005

Ahmed, Akbar. *Discovering Islam: Making Sense of Muslim History and Society (Revised Edition).* London: Routledge, 2002

Alexander, Peter. *Shakespeare's Life and Art.* New York University Press, 1961

Aligarh Muslim University, *List of Medal Recipients, 62nd Annual Convocation, 2014.* Retrieved on May 5, 2015 from http://www.amu.ac.in/convocation/pdf/medal2014.pdf

Archibald Henderson. 'Henry Arthur Jones, Dramatist: Self-Revealed'. *Virginia Quarterly Review,* [from University of Virginia], Autumn 1925, p.321-337. Retrieved on September 4, 2014, from http://www.vqronline.org/essay/henry-arthur-jones-dramatist-self-revealed

Barkow, Jerome H.; Cosmides, Leda; & Tobby, John; (Ed.). *The Adapted Mind: Evolutionary Psychology and the Generation of Culture.* 1992. New York: Oxford University Press, 1995

Basile, Giambattista. *Giambattista Basile's "The Tale of Tales, or Entertainment for Little Ones".* Nancy L. Canepa (Tr.). Detroit: Wayne State University Press, 2007

Bhutto, Zulfikar Ali. *Awakening the People: a collection of articles, statements and speeches, 1966 – 1969.* N.D. Reproduced as PDF by Sani Panwhar. Retrieved on May 7, 2015 from http://bhutto.org/Acrobat/Awakening%20the%20people.pdf

Brontë, Charlotte. *Jane Eyre. A Norton Critical Edition.* Richard J. Dunn (Ed.). 1971. New York: W. W. Norton & Company, Inc., 2001

Childs, Peter; and Roger Fowler. *The Routledge Dictionary of Literary Terms.* Oxon: Routledge, 2006

Dar, Shaukat (Urdu). 'Waheed Murad se aik mulaqat' (Urdu: 'A meeting with Waheed Murad'). 1973. Feature published in the Urdu film magazine Mussawir and retrieved on May 6, 2015 from http://waheedmurad.weebly.com/interviews.html

Daram, Dr. Mahmoud; and Marziyeh S. Ghoreishi. *Shakespeare and Nezami.* Lahore: Iqbal Academy Pakistan, 2013

Ganjavi, Nezami. *The Story of Layla and Majnun.* R. Gelpke (Tr.). London: Bruno Cassirer Ltd., 1966

Gazdar, Mushtaq. *Pakistan Cinema, 1947-1997.* Karachi: Oxford University Press, 1997

Gazdar, Mushtaq. Pakistan Cinema. Karachi: Oxford University Press, 1997

Giddings, Franklin Henry. *Democracy and Empire with studies of their Psychological, Economic, and Moral foundations.* 1900. New York: The MacMillan Company, 1901

Giddings, Franklin Henry. *Inductive Sociology.* 1900. New York: The MacMillan Company, 1901

Gilbert, Stuart. *James Joyce's Ulysses.* New York: Vintage Books, 1955

Goethe, Johann Wolfgang von. *Autobiography: Truth and Fiction Relating to My Life.* John Oxenford. 1882. London: The Anthological Society, 1901

Goldsmith, Oliver. *She Stoops to Conquer.* Edited by Dudley Miles, Ph. D. (Columbia). Boston: Ginn and Company, 1917

Hali, Maulana Altaf Husain (Urdu). *Hayat-i-Javid* [The Eternal Life]. Lahore: Book Talk, 2007

Hali, Maulana Altaf Husain (Urdu). *Musaddas-i-Hali.* Karachi: Taj Company Ltd., n.d.

Hardin, James N. (Ed.). *Reflection and Action: Essays On the Bildungsroman.* Columbia: University of Carolina Press, 1999

Husain, Dr. Sultan Mahmood (Urdu). *Allama Iqbal kay Ustaad Shamsul Ulema Maulvi Syed Mir Hasan* [*The Teacher of Allama Iqbal, Shamsul Ulema Maulvi Syed Mir Hasan*]. Lahore: Iqbal Academy Pakistan, 1981

Innes, Christopher (Ed.). *The Cambridge Companion to George Bernard Shaw.* 1998. Cambridge: Cambridge University Press, 2004

Iqbal, Dr. Sir Muhammad (Urdu). *Kulliyat-i-Iqbal Urdu* [Complete Poetical Works of Iqbal in Urdu]. Lahore: Iqbal Academy Pakistan, 1990

Iqbal, Dr. Sir Muhammad ['Allama Muhammad Iqbal']. *Discourses of Iqbal.* Shahid Husain Razzaqi (Ed.). 1979. Lahore: Iqbal Academy Pakistan, 2003

Iqbal, Dr. Sir Muhammad ['Iqbal'] (Persian). *Kulliyat-i-Iqbal Urdu* [Complete Poetical Works of Iqbal in Urdu]. 1990. Lahore: Iqbal Academy Pakistan, 1994

Iqbal, Dr. Sir Muhammad. (Urdu). *Anwar-i-Iqbal* [The Illuminations of Iqbal]. Bashir Ahmad Dar (Ed.). 1967. Lahore: Iqbal Academy Pakistan, 1977

Iqbal, Dr. Sir Muhammad. *The Letters of Iqbal.* B. A. Dar (Ed.). Lahore: Iqbal Academy Pakistan, 1978

Iqbal, Dr. Sir Muhammad. *Speeches, Writings and Statements of Iqbal* (Third Edition). Latif Ahmad Sherwani (Ed.). 1977. Lahore: Iqbal Academy Pakistan, 1995

Iqbal, Dr. Sir Muhammad. *Stray Reflections, the Private Notebook of Muhammad Iqbal; also includes: 'Stray Thoughts'.* Dr. Javid Iqbal (Ed.). 1961. Lahore: Iqbal Academy Pakistan, 2006

Iqbal, Mazhar. *Pakistan Film Magazine* (Website). Last visited by the present author on May 7, 2015 at http://mazhar.dk/film/

Jamil, Raju. 'Some are old and some are new' [thread posted by him with the nick 'Arjay' in October 2008]. Retrieved on April 25, 2015 from http://www.paklinks.com/gs/video-gallery/295630-some-are-old-and-some-are-new-by-arjay-4.html

Jinnah, Fatima. *Speeches, Messages and Statements of Madar-i-Millat Mohtarama Fatima Jinnah (1948-1967).* Salahuddin Khan (Ed.). Lahore: Research Society of Pakistan, 1976

Joyce, James. *A Portrait of the Artist as a Young Man.* New York: B. W. Heubsch, 1916

Joyce, James. *Ulysses.* 1922. London: Penguin, 2000

Jyotika Virdi. *The Cinematic ImagiNation: Indian Popular Films as Social History.* New Brunswick: Rutgers University Press, 2003

Karim, Saleena. *Secular Jinnah & Pakistan: What the Nation Doesn't Know.* Co. Mayo (Ireland): Checkpoint Press, 2010

Khan, Adeel A. 'Shades of glory: Sohail Rana'. *Dawn,* April 19, 2009. Retrieved on April 25, 2015 from http://www.dawn.com/news/921154/shades-of-glory-sohail-rana

Khan, Nawab Sir Zulfiqar Ali. *A Voice from the East.* 1922. Lahore: Iqbal Academy Pakistan, 1982

Leo Braudy & Marshall Cohen, ed. *Film Theory and Criticism: Introductory Readings (Seventh Edition).* 1974. New York: Oxford University Press, 2009

Mahmood, Namrah. *The Caravan of Light.* Blog at caravanoflight.blogspot.com

Manto, Saadat Hasan. Kingdom's End and Other Stories. Translated by Khalid Hasan. London: Verso, 1987

Michie, Elsie B. (Ed.). *Charlotte Brontë's Jane Eyre: A Casebook.* New York: Oxford University Press, 2006

Mukherjee, Meenakshi. *Early Novels in India.* 2002. New Delhi: Sahitya Academy, 2005

Nadvi, Syed Sulaiman (Urdu). *Khilafat Aur Hindustan* (Urdu: Caliphate and India). Azamgarh: Matbaa Muarif, 1340 A.H. [1922]

Najam, S. A. (Urdu). *Waheed Murad Ka Qatil Kaun* (Urdu: 'Who Killed Waheed Murad). Karachi: Crescent Academy, n.d.

Nichols, Beverley. *The Verdict on India.* London: Jonathan Cape Ltd., 1944

Noorani, Asif. 'A Gentleman Director'. *Dawn Images,* November 29, 2008. Retrieved on April 27, 2015 from http://www.dawn.com/news/860254/obituary-farewell-pervez-malik

Noorani, Asif. 'Those were the days'. *N.D.* Retrieved on April 27, 2015 from http://www.musicpakistan.net/modules.php? name =News&file=article&sid=160

Oxenford, John (Tr.). *Conversations of Goethe with Eckermann and Soret* (Revised Edition). London: George Bell & Sons, 1883.

Passport of Nisar Murad. AC163966 issued by order of the President Pakistan, April 3, 1965

Passport of Nisar Murad. AE949260 issued by order of the President Pakistan, August 7, 1976

Passport of Waheed Murad. AE402464 issued by order of the President Pakistan, September 24, 1975

Pirrault, Charles. *The Complete Fairy Tales.* Christopher Betts (Tr.). Oxford: Oxford University Press, 2009

Rashid, Hashim Bin; and Sher Khan. 'Goonda Raj: the reald-life characters behind the Goonda and Gandasa Era of Lollywood'. *The Express Tribune Magazine,* November 25 – December 1, 2012, pp.20-26

Rousseau, Jean-Jacques. *The Social Contract and The First and Second Discourses.* Edited and with an Introduction by Susan Dunn; with essays by Gita May, Robert N. Bellah, David Bromwich, Conor Cruise O' Brien. New Haven: Yale University Press, 2002

Shafique, Khurram Ali. 'Women and Cinema in Pakistan'. *The News International: You* (Vol. 3; No. 11), 1993 (a)

— 'The Chocolate-Cream Hero Legend'. *The Star,* May 20, 1993 (b)

— 'The Rise and Fall of Cult Heroes'. *Dawn Tuesday Review,* October 24-30, 1995 (a)

— 'The Importance of Being Eve'. *Dawn Tuesday Review,* October 31 – November 6, 1995 (b)

— 'Sold for a Song'. *Dawn Tuesday Review,* November 7-13, 1995 (c)

— 'The Director's Cut.' Dawn Tuesday Review, Nov 14-20, 1995 (d)

— 'The Hunt for Success'. *Dawn Tuesday Review,* November 21-27, 1995 (e)

— 'Profile: Sohail Rana'. *Dawn Tuesday Review*, January 23-29, 1996 (a)
— 'Profile: Pervez Malik.' *Dawn Tuesday Review*, August 20-26, 1996 (b)
— 'Profile: Nisar Bazmi'. *Dawn Tuesday Review,* October 29-November 4, 1996 (c)
— 'Profile: Syed Afzal Hussain.' *Herald,* July 1997
— 'Romeo and Juliet: an Immortal Love Story'. *Dawn Images,* August 21, 2005 (a)
— 'The Onscreen Love of Shirin Farhad'. *Dawn Images*, November 20, 2005 (b)
— *The Republic of Rumi: a Novel of Reality.* Lahore: Iqbal Academy Pakistan, 2007 (a)
— *The Beast and the Lion.* Lahore: Iqbal Academy Pakistan, 2007 (b)
— *Iqbal: An Illustrated Biography.* 2006. Lahore: Iqbal Academy Pakistan, 2007 (c)
— 'The Mystery behind Waheed Murad'. *Dawn Images,* November 23, 2008 (a)
— 'Farewell, Pervez Malik'. *Dawn Images,* November 30, 2008 (b)
— 'Armaan of a nation'. *Dawn Images,* March 14, 2010 (a)
— 'A portrait of the artist as Waheed Murad'. *Nukta Art Mag,* Vol. 5, Issue 2; October 2010 (b)
— 'Samandar: a Parable?'. *Dawn Images,* November 28, 2010 (c)
— *Shakespeare According to Iqbal.* Lahore: Iqbal Academy Pakistan, 2010 (d)
— 'Breaking down the wall'. *The Express Tribune Sunday Magazin,* November 11, 2012 (b)
— 'Sohni Dharti: From Heer Ranjha to the gandasa'. *The Express Tribune Sunday Magazin,* November 25, 2012 (c)
— *2017: The Battle for Marghdeen.* Nottingham: Libredux Publishing, 2012 (a)
— *Iqbal: His Life and Our Times.* Nottingham: Libredux Publishing, 2014
Shafique, Khurram Ali (Urdu). *Irtabat-e-Harf-o-Maani.* Lahore: Iqbal Academy Pakistan, 2007
— (Urdu). *Iqbal, Ibtidai Daur* [Iqbal, the Early Period]. Lahore: Iqbal Academy Pakistan, 2008
— (Urdu). *Iqbal, Tashkeeli Daur* [Iqbal, the Formative Period]. Lahore: Iqbal Academy Pakistan, 2010
— (Urdu). *Psycho Mansion.* Karachi: Fazlee Sons, 2011 (a)
— (Urdu). *Rana Palace.* Karachi: Fazlee Sons, 2011 (b)
— (Urdu) *Iqbal, Darmiani Daur* [Iqbal, the Middle Period]. Lahore: Iqbal Academy Pakistan, 2012
— (Urdu). *Kitab-i-Urdu: Chhati Jamaat Ke Liye* [The Urdu Book for Class 6]. Karachi: Topline Publishers, 2015 (a)

— (Urdu). *Kitab-i-Urdu: Satveen Jamaat Ke Liye* [The Urdu Book for Class 7]. Karachi: Topline Publishers, 2015 (b)

— (Urdu). *Kitab-i-Urdu: Aathveen Jamaat Ke Liye* [The Urdu Book for Class 8]. Karachi: Topline Publishers, 2015 (c)

Shakespeare, William. *The Taming of the Shrew* [Third Series of the Arden Edition of the Works of William Shakespeare]. Edited by Brian Morris. 1981. London: Thomson Learning, 2003

Shaw, [George] Bernard. *Arms and the Man: A Pleasant Play.* 1898. New York: Brentano's, 1913

Shvetal Vyas. 'The disappearance of Muslim socials in Bollywood'. University of South Australia, 2011. Retrieved April 25, 2015 from http://www.unisa.edu.au/ Documents/ EASS/ MnM/commentaries/vyas-muslim-socials.pdf

Sudhir Kakar. *Intimate Relations: Exploring Indian Sexuality.* Chicago: Chicago University Press, 1989

Syed Sulaiman Nadvi, *Khilafat Aur Hindustan* (Caliphate and India; in Urdu), pp.84, etc.

Taylor, A. J. P. *English History 1914-45.* [First published as *The Oxford History of England,* Vol. 15]. 1965. Oxford: Oxford University Press, 2001

Ter Ellingson. *The Myth of the Noble Savage.* Berkeley: University of California Press, 2001

Thornton, Weldon. *Allusions in Ulysses: a line-by-line Reference to Joyce's Complex Symbolism.* 1961. New York: Simon and Schuster, 1973

Walker, Michael. *Hitchcock's Motifs.* Amsterdam: Amsterdam University Press, 2005

Watt, Ian. *The Rise of the Novel.* California: University of California Press, 1957

Electronic resources

The interview of Waheed Murad in the PTV show *Silber Jubilee* (1983). Retrieved from YouTube on April 25, 2015. Complete URLs: https://youtu.be/YxYKkVlhnOs and https://youtu.be/CLxO7V6rxkg

The interview of Nazir Ali in PTV show *Mithrey Geet* (Punjabi). Retrieved from YouTube on April 25, 2015. Complete URL: https://youtu.be/8vZi-8bgdfc

'Inspirational message from Sohail Rana'. Published by the present author on YouTube on July 16, 2014 https://www.youtube.com/watch?v=8j7_3pOG_-Q

Interviews in Person

Between 1984 and the completion of this book, I had the chance to meet several people who had met Waheed Murad, including the following who have been quoted in the book.

Commodore (retired) Qaisar Mahmood (late), a grandson of Zahoor Ilahi Murad. I was first introduced to him in emails in 2011 through the courtesy of Adil Murad. I later interviewed him in Lahore on September 12, 2013. He checked the relevant portions of the draft (relating to the history of the Murad family) through email later the same month.

Javid Ali Khan, the best friend of Waheed Murad since their childhood. I was first introduced to him in Karachi in 1996 through the courtesy of Mrs. Salma Murad. He kindly gave me a detailed interview at that time, and two more in 2008.

Syed Iqbal Hussain Rizvi (credited in movies as Iqbal Rizvi), colleague of Waheed Murad. He kindly gave me a very long interview in Lahore on January 17, 2014

Mrs. Salma Murad, the widow of Waheed Murad. Since 1996, Mrs. Murad has very kindly been providing information and support for this project.

Sohail Rana, colleague of Waheed Murad. I interviewed him twice in 1993 for his profile written by me for *Dawn Tuesday Review*, published in 1996 and cited in the textual sources. In 2008, I communicated with him indirectly through Moosa Reza, the administrator of the website sohailrana.com

Pervez Malik, colleague of Waheed Murad. I interviewed him first in Islamabad in 1996, and then twice again in Karachi the next year. Part of my findings was incorporated into his profile written by me for *Dawn Tuesday Review*, published in 1996 and cited in the textual sources.

The End

... but there is more at www.waheedmurad.com

www.ingramcontent.com/pod-product-compliance
Lightning Source LLC
LaVergne TN
LVHW051408080426
835508LV00022B/2986